SALVATION HISTORY

SALVATION
HISTORY

AN INTRODUCTION TO BIBLICAL THEOLOGY

NEAL M. FLANAGAN, O.S.M.

Sheed Andrews and McMeel, Inc.
Subsidiary of Universal Press Syndicate
Kansas City

© Sheed & Ward, Inc., 1964

Library of Congress Catalog Card Number 64-19902

ISBN: 0-8362-0069-1

IMPRIMI POTEST
    Fr. Joseph M. Loftus, O.S.M.
    Provincial Prior
    Province of Our Lady of Sorrows

NIHIL OBSTAT
    Brendan Lawlor
    Censor Deputatus

IMPRIMATUR
    ✠ Robert F. Joyce
    Bishop of Burlington
    June 13, 1964

The Nihil Obstat and Imprimatur are a declaration that a book or pamphlet is considered to be free from doctrinal or moral error. It is not implied that those who have granted the Nihil Obstat and Imprimatur agree with the contents, opinions or statements expressed.

Sheed Andrews and McMeel, Inc.
6700 Squibb Road
Mission, Kansas 66202

Manufactured in the United States of America

To Monsignor Edwin M. Kinch, O.S.M.
First Prefect-Apostolic of the Servite Missions in Zululand
and to his wonderful African nuns
who brought this book into existence.

FOREWORD

THIS BOOK is an African child, born in the beautiful hill-town of Hlabisa, Zululand. There I attempted to present to a most attentive group of African nuns, catechists, and mission-school teachers one of the unifying themes of the Bible, that of *Man's Salvation*. In the year that followed, the same material was given to university students, to Irish Dominican nuns, and to the novices and philosophers of the Servite House of Studies in Benburb, Ireland. It is now offered in book form to similar nonspecialists, to all Christians interested in deepening their knowledge of the Bible and its basic teachings.

This volume does not pretend to be a commentary on the whole of the Bible, nor an exhaustive treatment on any one part of it. It is, rather, a primer of biblical theology, centered on the one theme of *Man's Salvation*.

The Old Testament citations from 1–4 Kings (Samuel and Kings), 1–2 Chronicles, Ezra, and Nehemia are taken from the *Revised Standard Version of the Bible*, copyrighted 1946 and 1952 by the Division of Christian Education, National Council of Churches, and used by permission. All other Old Testament citations come from the new *Confraternity of Christian Doctrine* translation. The translations of 1 Corinthians 10,16–17 and James 5,14–15 are my own. All other New Testament texts are quoted from the *New English Bible* with permission of the copyright holders: Oxford and Cambridge University Presses. The quotation from Daniel-Rops' *Israel and the Ancient World* is made with the kind permission of the publishers, Eyre & Spottiswoode.

The author owes a debt of gratitude to countless scholars whose books, lectures, and articles have given him whatever grasp of biblical theology he possesses. In particular he proclaims his grateful thanks to Fathers Pierre Benoit, O.P. and Stanislas Lyonnet, S.J. who passed on to him a share in their own priceless treasure — an enthusiastic appreciation of St. Paul. Finally, thanks are sincerely offered to Father Robert O'Keefe, O.S.M. whose critique of the typescript eliminated a host of grammatical mishaps.

N. M. F.

CONTENTS

SALVATION HISTORY

PART I

OLD TESTAMENT PREPARATION FOR SALVATION

1

CREATION-MAN-SIN

(Read Genesis, Chapters 1–11)

WHEN THE LAWYER asked Jesus what must be done to obtain eternal life, Jesus answered: "What is written in the Law? What is your reading of it?" And the lawyer replied: "'Love the Lord your God with all your heart, with all your soul, with all your strength, and with all your mind; and your neighbour as yourself.' 'That is the right answer,' said Jesus; 'do that and you will live.' But he wanted to vindicate himself, so he said to Jesus, 'And who is my neighbour?'" Jesus answered this important question by telling the story which begins with the now familiar words: "A man was on his way from Jerusalem down to Jericho when he fell in with robbers, who stripped him, beat him, and went off leaving him half dead" (Luke 10, 25–30). This, as we recognize, is the parable of the Good Samaritan. To the lawyer's question Jesus answers with a story. In vivid fashion it tells us that all men, even our natural enemies, must be considered as our neighbours, and that our love and mercy must be extended especially to him who needs help the most.

On another occasion (Luke 15,11ff.), Jesus told the story of the man with the two sons, the younger of whom demanded his inheritance and then proceeded to waste it on wine, women, and song. As fast as his money ran out so did his friends. Finally the poor chap was reduced to tending pigs, feeding them slops of food better even than he himself had to eat. At last he returned to his home and to the forgiving love of his father. This, of course, is the parable of the Prodigal Son. It tells us the most important and inspiring truth ever revealed to mankind: *God loves men,* and His arms are wide open to receive them back from the swinish diet of their repented sins.

The question I would like to pose here is this: Are the parables of the Good Samaritan and of the Prodigal Son *true?* This will serve to introduce the problem of truth in literature, one which is not quite so simple as might be imagined.

The concept of truth has a somewhat different meaning according to the type of literature to which it is applied. The modern history book, for example, is true if its facts are correct, if its geography and chronology are exact, if its interpretation of the meaning and relationship of events is accurate. But what about poetry? Is there no truth to be found in it? And what of the parable? That, too, must have a truth of its own. What it is you can probably guess. A parable is true if what it teaches is true. And certainly what we are taught in the parables of the Good Samaritan and of the Prodigal Son is absolutely true. Every man *is* our neighbor, and God *does* love us.

Parables are not history. They are simple stories whose whole purpose is to teach some truth. Frequently they are much more important than any book of profane history ever written. The point is this: Jesus taught important truths through interesting and easily remembered simple tales. As we shall see immediately, the Old Testament writers often did the same.

Creation (*Read Genesis 1,1–2,3*)

The first chapter of the book of Genesis is familiar to us all. In rapid fashion we read that God created the world and then spent six days putting it into exact order, resting on the seventh day, the Sabbath. As we follow the description of the various works, we read that God first *divides* light from darkness. Next He *divides* waters above from waters below by means of a firmament, some kind of solid dome which pushes the primordial waters apart. This leaves water above the firmament (thus accounting for the rains) and water underneath it. In between is the air. On the third day God *divides* again, this time the earth from the water left below. The result: water above the celestial dome, the dome or firmament itself, the air immediately beneath it, and, at the bottom, the waters below with the earth jutting out from them.

On the fourth day God makes the sun and the moon and the stars. This is surprising since we had already been told about light on the first day, and surely the sun, moon and stars are related to light. In some way the fourth day must be related to the first.

On the fifth day the birds of the air and the fish of the sea make their appearance. This is also interesting since it carries the reader back to the work of the second day. At that time the firmament divided the world into the two areas of air and water. Now these same areas are decorated with their inhabitants, the air with birds, the water with fish. The fifth day, consequently, is related to the second.

If it be true that the work of the first day is related to that of the fourth, and the work of the second day to that of the fifth, it should follow that what happened on the third day has an echo in the work of the sixth. This is the case. On the third day the earth was separated from the waters below. On the sixth God creates the beasts and (finally) man who inhabit the earth. The work of the sixth day, therefore, does refer back to that of the third.

This simple consideration of the creation account shows clearly that the author has presented a very *artistic* description. The first three days speak of division; the last three of inhabitation. What

God divides on the first day, He ornaments on the fourth; what He divides on the second, He ornaments on the fifth; what He divides on the third, He ornaments on the sixth. Such artistic parallelism should make us think of poetic imagery rather than of prose history.

Other poetic elements are also evident. The same phrases run through the chapter like refrains in a song. God speaks, for example, "Let there be light," and the effect is immediate, "And so it was." God next sees that the effect is good. Then He names it. Evening and morning follow, another day. It is the constant repetition of the same phrases which gives us further cause to think of poetic artistry rather than of scientific writing.

This leads us to the conclusion that what we have here is a very artistic story, interesting, easily remembered. The parallelism of the works, the repetition of the phrases, make it the sort of account that could be heard once, remembered with little difficulty, and then passed on to any attentive audience. Its six-days-plus-the-Sabbath arrangement is that of the Jewish work week, for the author definitely intends to tell his fellow Jews that they must rest on the Sabbath just as God Himself is pictured as doing.

Another element that enters into this account is the fact that the author is not an experimental scientist recording historical facts. What he has in mind, as we shall see, is not science but theology, not a description of the physical construction of the universe, but of the nature and power of God and of the grandeur of man, earth's masterpiece. When he speaks of the world he does so in a non-scientific language, the language of appearances. The heavens, the sky, look like a dome so that is the way he describes them. He simply speaks of the world the way the people of his time and country were accustomed to describe it. If the twentieth century scientific explanations of the world's formation had been revealed to him he would have shrugged his shoulders. That was not his interest. He wanted to speak of God, and the language and concepts of his own time served him well enough for that. Besides, if he were to have been given exact scientific knowledge by God and had written it down, who among his own people would have understood him? The following diagram pictures the Jewish cosmogony used by the author and the work-parallelism which he follows:

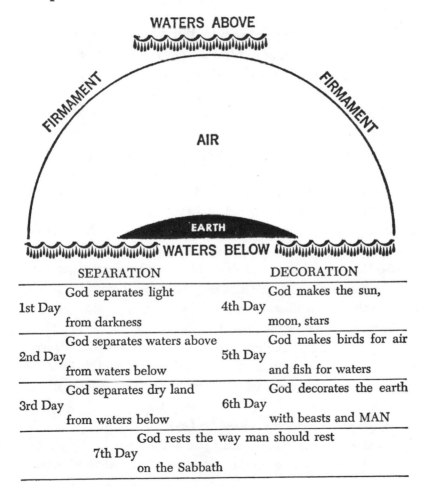

	SEPARATION		DECORATION
1st Day	God separates light from darkness	4th Day	God makes the sun, moon, stars
2nd Day	God separates waters above from waters below	5th Day	God makes birds for air and fish for waters
3rd Day	God separates dry land from waters below	6th Day	God decorates the earth with beasts and MAN
7th Day	God rests the way man should rest on the Sabbath		

Granting that our author is interested in theology and not physical science, and that his literary form is closer to poetry than to prose, the question rises very naturally: Is the story true? The answer must be that this chapter of Genesis is true, absolutely true, in the sense that a parable is true. What it teaches, and all that it teaches, is completely true. Even a partial list of the teachings in this one short account is impressive.

1—There is only one God, and all other things are His creatures.

2—God is a person, a living God of intellect and will. He is not some force of nature, not the sun, nor the moon, nor the flood. And, as a personal God, He can be loved and served with devotion.

3—God created the world from nothing. That this teaching is contained in our story is disputed. It may well be, however, that by the time this account was finally written down, perhaps in the sixth century B.C., the Jewish world believed in creation and that our author intended to teach it.

4—God is a God of order. The account is one of consummate order, and intends to teach its readers that this is the way that God acts.

5—Man has primacy in the animal world. He is mentioned last as the masterpiece of material creation. Only before his formation does God deliberate within Himself, and to man alone is dominion given over the animal world.

6—Man's dignity is that of a creature made to God's image and likeness. Being a creature of understanding and decision, he can exercise the power which is his over the creatures of the world.

7—Marriage is a state blessed by God.

8—Man should devote at least one day a week to God.

9—The world and everything in it were created GOOD. Proceeding from God's creative hand, they carried a touch of His GOODNESS with them.

These are no small truths. This one, short, extremely artistic and well balanced account reveals enough truth about God and man to furnish the basis of a deeply penetrating and extensive theology. Yet the full wisdom and magnificence of the story can be appreciated only when we realize that this description was meant to counteract another creation story, that of the pagans.

The pagan creation story of the Mesopotamian world begins with a male and female deity (sex is primeval). These beget numerous lesser deities. A battle ensues between the parents and their offspring. In the battle, the male god is killed, but the female goddess, Tiamat, lives on to war against the children. After a fierce fight she is killed. From her carcass are formed the sun, the moon, the stars. This is the pagan story. It tells little about the notions the pagans had regarding the world, but a great deal about the crude ideas they had of their deities.

We can imagine the Jews, to whom this pagan account was well known, violently shaking their heads and saying, "But that's not what God is like at all." So they told their own story about God, and this, in the course of time, was written down as chapter one of Genesis by the inspired author. It teaches that there are not many gods, but only one, and He a person Who should inspire our love and obedience. The created world is not the result of battles and savagery, but the well-ordered effect of God's supreme will, a will which demonstrates God's infinite power. Man is not the plaything of the gods, dependent upon their vulgar whims and fancies, but the human lord of creation and a mirror of God's perfections. Sex is not primeval, is not all-important, but is a blessing from God protected by the context of marriage. Man, though noble, is still only a creature, and, as such, should dedicate at least the Sabbath to the worship of his Creator. Finally, and this is a point very important for the theme of salvation, all things came from the hand of God clothed in GOODNESS. The world at this point stood in no need of salvation. Man was an intimate friend of God.

Man (*Read Genesis 2,4–25*)

With the second chapter of Genesis, verse four, a new and quite different account begins. "This is the story of the heavens and the earth at their creation." It tells us not so much about the creation of the world as about the formation of man and woman. In comparison with the first chapter of Genesis, it is much older and much more figurative and symbolic. This use of strongly figurative speech takes a bit of getting used to for the modern reader. It's not that we are being told whimsical fairy tales, but that the author is teaching profound truths in vivid and colorful language. What is necessary is that we pierce through the outer shell of the story to find the kernel which lies within. Take, for example, verses 19–20. In them we are told of a circus-like parade of animals before Adam. He names them as they pass, and at the end of the parade he has found none similar to himself. This is simply an animated description meant to teach in concrete fashion that man is lord of the animal world. According to the Semitic mentality of the time the *power to name* was possessed by the one with the power to rule. That is why Adam is pictured as naming the animals. He does not, you can note, name the sun, the moon, the stars, the day and night, because he has no power over them. It is God Who names those things. The story of the animal procession teaches another fact as well: among the animals of the earth none was human but man.

The author's frequent use of figurative speech must be kept in mind in reading this and the following chapter. Otherwise, we

will fail to discern his teaching and will attribute ideas to him
which he would be the first to repudiate. Centuries ago the
brilliant St. Augustine warned against too slavish an interpretation of the texts concerning man's formation wherein symbolic
expressions abounded. He cautioned against accepting things
which would seem ridiculous to unbelievers.

What, then, are we told about the formation of the first man
and woman? Adam is formed from *clay* and the *breath of God.*
The symbols here are evident. Man is different from the rest
of the animal world. He is composed of two elements. Matter is
the first. Clay is its symbol simply because man's body decom-
poses into the clay of the world and because the Hebrew word
for clay, *adamah,* is similar to the word for man, *adam.* The
second element is something vastly superior and less material,
human life, of which the breath of God is a striking symbol.
The teaching here is magnificent: man possesses a life, a vital
force, so verging on the divine that it can be called the breath
of God. Indeed the whole of the Judeo-Christian tradition is
based on a firm belief that man is essentially different from all
other living things. Though he is like God, he is not God: though
he is like the beasts, he is not one of them.

One other important truth is contained in this chapter: "It is
not good that the man is alone." His mate, his complement, is
developed by God. Made after the model of man himself, she
is meant to become one with him in marriage and to take her
place at his side (3,12). The chapter then concludes with a clear
reference to the GOODNESS of sex unmarred by sin, and to the
permanency of marriage. "She is now bone of my bone, and flesh
of my flesh; she shall be called Woman, for from man she has
been taken. For this reason a man leaves his father and mother,
and clings to his wife, and the two become one flesh. Both the
man and his wife were naked, but they felt no shame" (2,23-25).

Sin (*Read Genesis 3,1–11,26*)

The third chapter of Genesis is integrally united to the preceding account of the formation of man and woman. It introduces a new character, the tempter. This figure of evil whom the Apocalypse 12,9 and 20,2 identifies with Satan is portrayed as a serpent either because the people of ancient times attributed extraordinary wisdom to that beast, or because the serpent was a symbol of the coarse fertility rites which were the curse of the pagan world at that epoch. At any rate, the main teaching of the chapter is quite clear. Man rebelled against God through inordinate pride and deliberate disobedience. This rebellion is termed the eating of the fruit of the tree of knowledge of good and evil, which means a participation in an act which gave Adam and Eve a practical experience of what evil was. This might also mean simply that the sin was mixed up with an attempt on man's part to be the ultimate judge of what moral good and evil would be. We actually do not know the precise details of that first sin, nor is such knowledge necessary. The sad fact is that man did sin by rebelling against the will of God.

Punishment followed necessarily. Man's defiance of God brought not equality with God but a profound sense of shame. The gift of sex by which God had shared His creative power became disorganized. Nakedness became a disturbing element in man's constitution. Childbearing for women, so exalted by God earlier in Genesis became a mixed-blessing surrounded by pain. Man's rule over the earth became disputed, to be retained only by continual sweat and toil. Worst of all, man's intimate friendship with God became a thing of the past. How simply does our text state this: "the man and his wife hid themselves from the Lord God among the trees of the garden" (3,8).

And death, too, steps onto the human stage. "Dust you are and unto dust you shall return" is the Judge's verdict. Man has become mortal. As Paul would put it many centuries later: "through one man . . . sin entered the world, and through sin death" (Romans 5,12).

The fall of man has set loose upon the world a new force, Satan and his kingdom. The elements of the kingdom are SATAN himself, SIN bringing DEATH which is so often preceded by SICKNESS. What a frightful quartet: Satan, sin, death, sickness. *It is this which makes salvation a necessity.* Man has lost God and the GOODNESS of God. Satan's kingdom has been established on earth. From that, from Satan-sin-death-sickness, man needs salvation.

It is at this point that the prospect of salvation is announced. Genesis 3,15 gives a mysterious promise. It speaks of the enmity, the warfare, between the woman and Satan, between her seed and his. In some undefined manner the woman's seed shall wound the serpent's head, while the serpent shall wound the heel of its attacker. This is, indeed, a strange promise. A battle is assured. To whom will go the victory? Seemingly to the seed of the woman. His is the vantage point of position. He can grind the serpent's head, its most vital part, whereas the only vulnerable target he himself presents is the back of his foot. The whole atmosphere of the account tells us, also, to which side God will lend His aid, surely to man, His masterpiece.

The story of man's fall ends with the symbol of the cherubim guarding the entrance to the garden with a flaming sword. Our author is stating in striking fashion: what man has lost he cannot regain. Gone forever is the state of primitive innocence. We are all, individually, the best witnesses to the truth of that statement.

By the end of the third chapter of Genesis, then, the story of salvation is taking definite form. Man has fallen into the power of Satan's kingdom. Man, therefore, needs salvation. And a promise has been made, one which speaks of the days of battle ahead and of the critical point at which both Satan and mankind shall be injured, Satan in the head, man in the heel.

During the following eight chapters (4–11) the book of Genesis concentrates on one main topic, sin. The author intends to impress upon his readers the feeling that the forces of Satan have ruthlessly invaded the world, and that the whole family of man, not Adam and Eve alone, has fallen before them. One story follows another. Often the full meaning of an individual account is difficult or impossible to discover, yet the common theme which pervades all of them is clearly that of sin.

There is the narrative, first of all, of Cain killing Abel. Obviously this is a sin story. And it might well be that the account carries with it a special lesson. Once man sins against God, he begins to sin against his fellow man. Love God and you love your brother; hate God and soon your hands reach out to shed your brother's blood. Our author speaks, too, of the early appearance of sacrifice. It is presented as something natural to man, the result of man's essential need to indicate, externally, his devotion to the Lord Who made him.

The sin story of Cain and Abel is followed by that of the "sons of God" and the "daughters of men" in chapter six. The narrative is somewhat baffling to us, but its main teachings are not difficult to determine. It is, again, a sin story as is evident in verse three which speaks of sin diminishing the life-span of man. It is evident, likewise, in verse five which affirms that "the wickedness of man on the earth was great, and that man's every thought and all the inclinations of his heart were only evil." It is possible that the story intends to teach us yet another fundamental truth. The "sons of God" symbolize, seemingly, the good while the "daughters of men" symbolize the evil. The world, says our narrative, is a union, a marriage, of good and evil. The two are hopelessly intermingled. (Nuclear science, we might say, can turn a desert country into a garden; and it can do the opposite, too, just as easily.)

The third story is that of the flood (6,5–9,17). Here the emphasis is on *God's reaction to sin,* on His complete and active opposition to this one force in the world which can stand up and say, "I will not serve." It is in no way the story of a divine tyrant who inflicts evil on a defenseless world. Rather, it is the moving tale in human terms of a loving God Whose heart grows sick at the sight of the ugliness that sinful man has brought into the beauty of creation. The flood story is so widespread in ancient literature that it presumes an historical event, an exceptionally devastating deluge in the Mesopotamian world. There is some archaeological evidence to reinforce this presumption. With this account we are told that sin was spreading so fast that flood waters were necessary to wash away its grimy stain.

It would be a mistake, however, to pass over the consoling teaching that, notwithstanding the emphasis on sin, the biblical account is also reminding us continually that God remains interested, lovingly interested, in this human creature made to His own image and likeness. Man remains tied to God by the thread of God's mercy. We are told this in the recital of the Fall by the reference to the victory which it presumes that the seed of the woman will win. We are told it again when God is pleased with Abel in 4,5 and with Henoch in 5,22–24. Even Cain is taken into God's providential care. The mark of Cain is not a curse, but a symbol of the divine protection. Finally, the story of the flood is an account of the particular favor that Noe and his family find in the sight of God. The covenant account of chapter nine is really a promise to the reader of better days to come.

The emphasis on sin is still apparent in chapter eleven which speaks of the Tower of Babel. The sin of pride is the villain of this narrative, while the aim of the story is to describe the effects of sin. From sin germinate the seeds of disunity and confusion among men. The moral of the story should not be unfamiliar to us. We live in an age, in a year, in which the fragile grouping of the nations is organized in the United Nations building. What is it that threatens disunity and confusion there but pride on a national scale and disregard for God and His laws?

The presence of sin is symbolized, finally, by the lists of phenomenal ages attributed to the patriarchs in 5,1–6,3 and in 11, 10–26. Some of the figures have probably been distorted in the transmission of the text, but the general pattern is that the ages decrease from the beginning of each list to its end. This technique is another means of indicating the constant growth of sin, the basic cause of death. Life decreasing is a sign of sin increasing.

By the time we have finished these stories we should have the feeling that sin is growing by leaps and bounds, that man's need for salvation from this fantastically awesome force is increasing almost by the minute. This is precisely the impression that the author wants to create. It is against this dark background that he wishes to present the brilliant figure of Abraham (Abram), the "friend of God" and the Father of the Chosen People.

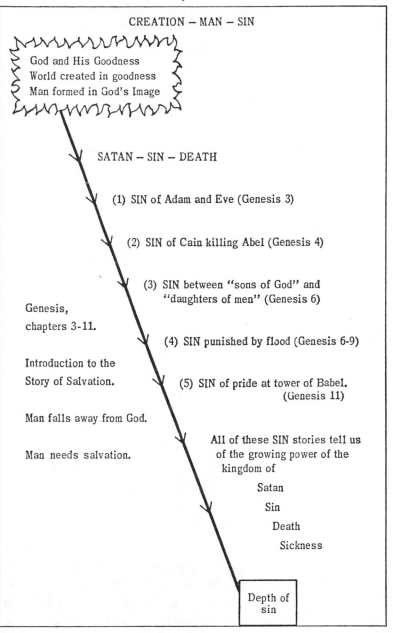

Chapter One

CREATION — MAN — SIN

God and His Goodness
World created in goodness
Man formed in God's Image

SATAN — SIN — DEATH

(1) SIN of Adam and Eve (Genesis 3)

(2) SIN of Cain killing Abel (Genesis 4)

(3) SIN between "sons of God" and "daughters of men" (Genesis 6)

Genesis, chapters 3-11.

(4) SIN punished by flood (Genesis 6-9)

Introduction to the Story of Salvation.

(5) SIN of pride at tower of Babel. (Genesis 11)

Man falls away from God.

Man needs salvation.

All of these SIN stories tell us of the growing power of the kingdom of

Satan

Sin

Death

Sickness

Depth of sin

2

FAMILY-PEOPLE-RELIGION

Family of Abraham (*Read Genesis, 12,1–25,8*)

AT THIS POINT the story of salvation moves considerably closer to what we might term "history" in the modern sense. We begin to deal with characters and events which can be determined in time, localized, placed within the context of general history.

The preceding nine chapters of Genesis (cc.3–11) have shown very vividly the force with which the kingdom of Satan fell upon man and the world in which he lived. *The movement has been away from God.* One sin story follows another, man falls farther and farther away from the original GOODNESS in which he was created: he falls farther and farther away from God. He needs salvation desperately, yet cannot provide it by himself. Is there even one man left faithful to his God?

And now, dramatically, God Himself steps in. He selects, from a world steeped in paganism, one small group of people, the clan of Thare that lives at Ur near the Persian Gulf, Ur of the Chaldees as it is often called. The clan moves up northwest to Haran near the source of the Euphrates River. From this clan God *elects* one man, Abraham. To this one man, the beginning of God's saving work and the beginning of the Chosen People, a revelation is made of the one God. The details of this first revelation are unknown, but it seems to have taken place before the famous

and important promises described in Genesis 12,1–3. These
promises treat Abraham as a man already intimate with his God.
The text is a moving one:

> The Lord said to Abram: 'Leave your country, your kinsfolk and
> your father's house, for the land which I will show you; I will make a
> great nation of you. I will bless you, and make your name great, so
> that you will be a blessing. I will bless them that bless you, and curse
> them that curse you. In you shall all the nations of the earth be
> blessed.'

That short text unfolds in a slightly generic form the *promises*
made freely by God to this man whom He has *elected* as the
vessel of salvation. In substance they speak of:

1—a *nation* which will come from Abraham;

2—a *land* which the nation will possess; and,

3—a blessing to be bestowed *on the nations of the earth* because of Abraham.

These promises are repeated in the chapters that follow, and
both the first and second of them will become more specific. The
land which will be given the posterity of Abraham will be that of
Canaan to the south-west of Haran, the land which later in history
was called Palestine. The prediction regarding the *nation* to
descend from Abraham is also made clearer. It is described as
enormous, as numerous as the dust-grains of the earth (13,16)
and the stars of the heavens (15,5). Even more important, it is
specified as a nation which will develop from a child of Abraham
—a child which Abraham will have through his old and sterile
wife, Sara. This is a promise which must have seemed almost incredible to him, yet that is what God predicted and that is what
Abraham had to believe. What was said in 12,3 with regard to
the nations being blessed in Abraham is repeated again in 18,18,
but it is never explained more clearly. It remained a mystery to
both Abraham and his posterity.

To confirm and seal these promises something like a *covenant*

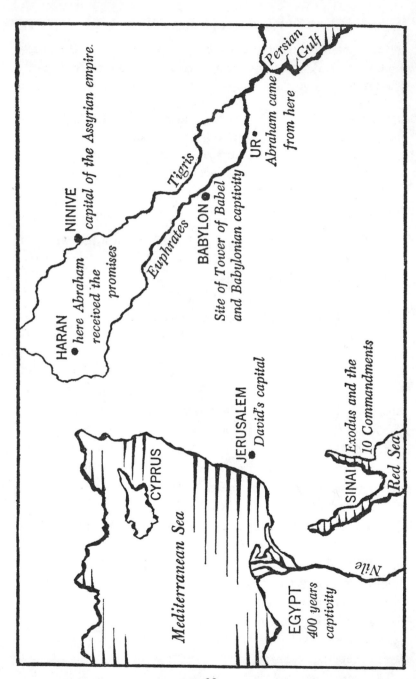

NINIVE
capital of the Assyrian empire.

HARAN
here Abraham
received the
promises

Tigris

Euphrates

BABYLON
Site of Tower of Babel
and Babylonian captivity

UR
Abraham came
from here

Persian Gulf

CYPRUS

Mediterranean Sea

JERUSALEM
David's capital

SINAI
Exodus and the
10 Commandments

Red Sea

EGYPT
400 years
captivity

Nile

is made between God and Abraham, this man of *election*. The covenant was an agreement, a pact, a religion, binding man to God. Chapter 15,17–18 describes an eerie scene. Abraham procures a heifer, a she-goat, a he-goat, a dove, and a young pigeon. These he cuts in two, placing the pieces opposite each other.

Now when the sun had set and it was dark, a smoking oven and a fiery torch passed between the pieces. On that day the Lord made a covenant with Abram, saying, 'To your posterity I will give this land . . .'

This covenant ritual follows the customs of the times. The parties entering the agreement passed through the severed animals to pledge themselves to similar destruction if they broke the pact. The external symbol of Abraham's new relationship, his new union, with God would be the rite of circumcision (17, 1–14).

What is important for the history of salvation in these accounts? The episodes in Abraham's life point out three aspects of the divine activity which will appear time and time again down the centuries as God brings salvation to the world. The first of these is *election*. God chooses whom He wills to be His instrument. On this occasion it is Abraham, an insignificant man from an insignificant clan from an insignificant town. Why Abraham? Because God wants him. That is the only possible answer. And so it will be down through the centuries. God chooses as He wishes: this man and not that, this man and not his brother. Isaac is chosen over Ismael, Jacob over Esau, Joseph over his brothers, Mary over all the virgins of Israel. The choice is always God's alone.

The second element is *promise*. The Old Testament is one of promise from beginning to end. At this moment promises are made to Abraham. They will be followed by many others made to later individuals whom God will elect as men of destiny. God need not make definite offers of future gifts, but He does, and His fidelity to His promises assures their fulfillment.

The third element is *covenant,* the divinely initiated union between God and man. The covenant with Abraham is a very simple one, but it does constitute the beginning at least of a religion, a binding of God to man and of man to God. The full-fledged religion of Israel was still some six centuries off in the future. In relation to this covenant with Abraham, it would be well to note that sacrifice enters in as one of its constituent parts.

These three elements of *election, promise, covenant* view Abraham's relation with God from the divine side. These are the things that God provides. Is there anything that Abraham himself offers? What is the response that he makes to God? *Faith!* Abraham believes, and with that the work of salvation begins on the part of man. He believes that God will give his posterity the land of Canaan (Palestine). He believes that he will have a posterity, one as numerous as the grains of dust and the stars of the heavens. Even more, he believes that God can and will raise up from the dead womb of the aged and sterile Sara a child who will be the beginning of his *family* and *nation.* This was not an easy promise to believe in. Sara laughed when she was told the news (18,12) and Abraham himself, man of faith though he was, chuckled at his first hearing of the glad tidings (17,17). It was a difficult promise, this, a hard saying, yet Abraham did believe. Because he did, his child was born to Sara. The boy's name, Isaac, is related to the Hebrew word for laughter, the laughter with which the promise of his birth was first received.

Isaac grew straight and strong, the idol of his father's heart and the apple of his eye. In this child lay the world's hope for salvation. Yet, when God tells Abraham to offer the boy as a holocaust, he marches off to the place of sacrifice brokenhearted but obedient. God halts his hand and restores his son to him, but only after Abraham has given further proof of a faith unequaled in the history of pre-Christian men. Little wonder, then, that St. Paul presents him as the model for Christian believers, and gives faith so prominent a role in the work of salvation. Just as the salvation of the whole world began with Abraham's belief, so does the salvation of the individual Christian begin with his belief, with his willingness to accept God's instructions and God's promises.

Can we date Abraham and set him and his life story in the context of profane history? Scholars agree today that the account of Abraham fits perfectly into what is known of the Mesopotamian and Canaanite world of the early second millennium B.C. The type of life and social customs attributed to Abraham and his family are similar to those which archaeology has determined for the semi-nomads of the time who were migrating in large numbers from Mesopotamia into Canaan. If we date Abraham about 1850 or 1800 B.C. we will not be far wrong.[1]

The family history of Abraham continues in the stories of Isaac and Jacob. (Read Genesis, chapters 21–36.) Isaac is described with faint lines, mainly in relation to his father Abraham and son Jacob, both strong personalities who dim the figure of Isaac into obscurity. However, God's renewal to Isaac of the promises made to Abraham is important to the history of salvation. In 26,3–5 God says to Isaac:

I will fulfill the oath which I swore to your father Abram. I will make your descendants as numerous as the stars of the heavens. I will give your descendants all these lands, and in your descendants all the nations of the earth shall be blessed. . . .

1. For pictures of the existing ruins of Ur, Haran, and Hebron, cf. Grollenberg's *Atlas of the Bible* (New York, Thomas Nelson & Sons, 1957), pp. 32–33. In the same volume note the picture atop p. 38. This is a painting, almost contemporaneous with Abraham, of a Semite family arriving in Egypt with a cargo of cosmetics, black paint for the eyes. Abraham and his family would not have differed much from that group.

Isaac's wife was Rebecca, selected not from the dwellers of Canaan but from relatives of his own family still living up north in Haran. Her first childbirth resulted in twin boys, Esau and Jacob. God, for some divine reason which we cannot attempt to understand, elected the second son, Jacob, in preference to the first, Esau. The character of Jacob is painted in very frank and unflattering colors. His purchase of the hungry Esau's birthright for a bowl of pea-soup (25,29–34) was crafty and mean, but not deceitful. The author is not nearly so displeased with Jacob's procedure on this occasion as with Esau's: "Thus lightly did Esau value his birthright" (25,34).

Jacob's trick of passing himself off as Esau to obtain his father's blessing (Genesis, chapter 27) seems unmitigated deceit, unless his possession of the birthright be some sort of explanation and apology. It is an instance of God writing straight with crooked lines, because through Jacob and not Esau will the plan of salvation continue.

Up to this point Jacob has shown the shabby side of his character. Once he has fled north to Haran to escape his brother's anger, however, a growth and deepening of his good traits become apparent. Genesis 28,10–22 tells of his vision and vow to God at Bethel, and of the renewal to him of the promises already made to Abraham and Isaac. Genesis 32,25–31 speaks of a further divine encounter and blessing at Phanuel, after which Jacob's name is changed to *Israel*. Both of these descriptions are meant to be indications of Jacob's advance in virtue. The beautiful account of his affection for Rachel and of the seven years he worked for her hand, years which "seemed to him but a few days because of his love for her" (Genesis 29,20), gives us the first love story in the biblical writings and a view of admirable human characteristics. Jacob remains a clever man in his dealings with Laban, an equally clever father-in-law, but the days of deceit are gone forever.

It was Laban, you may recall, who outmaneuvered Jacob in the marriage dealings for Rachel. We read that "Laban had two daughters. The elder was called Lia, and the younger Rachel. Lia's eyes were weak, but Rachel was shapely and beautiful" (Genesis 29,16–17). Jacob's gaze was attracted, not to the less-favored Lia, but to Rachel, that vision of pure delight, and it was for her hand that he slaved away during those seven years which passed as a day. On the night of the wedding celebration there was wine and good cheer in abundance, but when Jacob awoke in the morning he found that Lia, not Rachel, was nestled at his side. It's just an old family custom, explained Laban to his angry son-in-law. "It is not the custom in our country to give the younger daughter before the first-born; complete the week of this one's nuptials and I will give you the other in return for another seven years of service with me" (Genesis 29,26–27). Jacob, the clever one, had met his master.

Jacob's two wives, Rachel and Lia, and their two maids, Bala and Zelpha, give him twelve sons through whom God's saving plan will continue. Of these sons the most important turns out to be Joseph, son of Rachel and brother of Benjamin.

The story of Joseph (read Genesis, chapters 37–50) is one of the best known and most popular in the Old Testament. Sold into Egypt as a slave by his envious brothers, he proves to be a model of virtue and of wisdom. He rises to a position second only to that of the Pharao of the land. When his brothers come to Egypt looking for food during a period of famine, Joseph receives them with charity and kindness, a fine example, some 1700 years before its time, of the law of love given in Christ's Sermon on the Mount. Finally, the whole family of Jacob moves down into Egypt with Joseph, and there Jacob "drew up his feet into the bed and expired. And he was gathered to his people" (Genesis 49,33).

Such are the details of the story. Behind these facts, however, lies a great deal of Egyptian history and of divine planning. The rise of Joseph in Egyptian politics seemed for centuries to lend an aura of fairy-tale glamour to the account. How was it conceivable for a man to rise from slavery to so exalted a position in the government? We now know that from about 1700–1570 B.C. Egypt was overrun by Semite invaders from the north who captured control of the government. These foreigners were called "Hyksos," which means "chieftains of foreign lands." The military success of the Hyksos was due to their use of war horses and chariots, at that time not yet part of the Egyptian arsenal. All of this makes the rise of Joseph much more understandable. He rose as a foreigner in politics dominated by foreigners like himself.

Our author, of course, is not at all interested in the intriguing role which the Hyksos played in Egyptian history. His interest lies elsewhere, in the marvelous workings of God's providence. Salvation, remember, lies in the family of Jacob. During the bitter famine in Canaan this family is in danger of dying out. But it doesn't — simply because God has seen to it that one of the family, Joseph, is in a position important enough to keep the family alive. This is the reason why Joseph was sold into Egypt. How wonderful the ways of God's providence. Joseph's words tell the whole divine meaning of this episode.

I am your brother Joseph whom you sold into Egypt. Do not be distressed or angry with yourselves that you sold me here; for *God has sent me before you to save life.* For two years now the famine has been in the land, and for five more years there will be neither plowing nor reaping. God sent me before you *to preserve a remnant for you in the land, and to deliver you in a striking way.* Not you but God sent me here, and made me a father to Pharao, lord of all his house, and ruler over all the land of Egypt (Genesis 45,4–8).

The final chapters of Genesis are concerned with the deaths of Jacob-Israel and Joseph. Before Jacob-Israel dies he adopts two sons of Joseph, Ephraim and Manasse, as his own children. Of these two, Ephraim, though the younger, receives the greater blessing since his tribe will become the more important one in Canaan. The twelve tribes of Israel will be formed from Jacob-Israel's twelve sons, minus Joseph and Levi, plus Ephraim and Manasse. Joseph is subtracted because his two sons Ephraim and Manasse take his place. Levi is also eliminated because his descendants, the Levites, will become the ministers of the altar and live mainly from that.

As we come to the end of the book of Genesis it might be a help to summarize rapidly what has happened thus far in the history of salvation. The world and man were created in GOOD-NESS. Then came Satan and his kingdom: sin, death, sickness. Chapters 4–11 impressed us with the power of sin. In the 12th chapter Abraham was elected by God, received the promises and the covenant. The salvation of the human race started at that point. The promises were renewed to Isaac and to Jacob-Israel, and they followed the example of Abraham in dedicating themselves and their families to God through sacrifice. Finally Joseph was chosen to preserve the family which then moved down into Egypt

Family Grows into People (*Read Exodus, chapters 1–18*)

Now Joseph and all his brothers and that whole generation died. But the Israelites were fruitful and prolific. They became so numerous and strong that the land was filled with them. Then a new king, who knew nothing of Joseph, came to power in Egypt. He said to his subjects, 'Look how numerous and powerful the Israelite people are growing, more so than we ourselves! Come, let us deal shrewdly with them to stop their increase; otherwise, in time of war they too may join our enemies to fight against us, and so leave our country.' Accordingly, taskmasters were set over the Israelites to oppress them with forced labor. Thus they had to build for Pharao the supply cities of Phithom and Rameses. Yet the more they were oppressed, the more they multiplied and spread. The Egyptians, then, dreaded the Israelites and reduced them to cruel slavery, making life bitter for them with hard work in mortar and brick and all kinds of field work — the whole cruel fate of slaves (Exodus 1,6–14).[2]

In these few verses the book of Exodus, the second book of the Bible, compresses the history of some 400 years, leaping from Joseph to Moses. The downgrading of the Israelites, the descendants of Jacob-Israel, must have coincided with the fall of the Hyksos power in Egypt. These foreign invaders were overcome by the native Egyptians in the first half of the 16th century B.C. (about 1570), and we can well imagine the Israelites falling rapidly from favor after the expulsion of their Semite cousins. They continued to increase, however, forming what might be termed a very populous and inter-related family. When their fortune seemed to have reached its lowest depth, a deliverer, a savior, was sent to them. This was Moses, surely the outstanding figure in the whole of the Old Testament.

The infancy and young manhood of Moses were highlighted by his escape from death as a small child, his education in the court of the Pharao, his discovery of his true family background, his flight from Egypt after slaying an Egyptian who was persecuting an Israelite, and his arrival in the country of Madian. This latter was located to the south of Edom and to the east of the Gulf of Aqaba. At this point the truly important part of his life begins.

In the 3rd chapter of Exodus we read the story of Moses and

2. Cf. cut in Grollenberg's *Atlas*, p. 46.

the bush which burnt but was not consumed. Feet bared, for the place on which he stood was made holy by the presence of God, Moses was called by God to be the savior of the Hebrew slaves. To him was given the power of God to impress the Pharao, and also the revelation of God's name, *Yahweh*. The meaning of this name is disputed among scholars, but one well-founded opinion interprets it as "I am (He) who brings (things) into being." Moses consequently returned to Egypt and began negotiations with the Pharao for the release of the Israelites. The plagues, nature in revolt, pressured the Pharao toward this liberation, but he resisted until overcome by the last of the disasters, the death of the Egyptians' first-born. On the evening before this happened, the Israelites were told to slaughter a lamb for every family group, to sprinkle their doors with its blood, to eat in haste, ready for a sudden departure. The death which touched the first-born of the Egyptians *passed* harmlessly *over* the blood-sprinkled doors of the Israelites. This was the first *passover*, the crucial moment of liberation, a moment which was never forgotten in the centuries that followed. Pharao's hand was forced, he allowed the slaves to depart.

Out into the desert to the east fled the Israelites. There was a direct and short route into the land of Canaan, the goal of the fugitives, but Moses refused to take it. Perhaps it was obvious to him that a route which was speedy for him and his followers would be even speedier for the war chariots of the Pharao in case that vacillating tyrant changed his mind. And, in fact, Pharao did just that. All nations, one can suppose, part with the luxury of slave labor with considerable reluctance. Pharao's forces pursued the Israelites, caught up to them, but then were annihilated by the rapid closing of the waters of the Red Sea which, through some divinely instigated phenomenon of nature, had permitted the passage of the Israelites. This was a second divine act (the passover was the first) which these escaped slaves and their descendants never forgot. By such prodigies of power did Yahweh their God rescue them from the most powerful empire of that time. By such prodigies did Yahweh reveal His power, His mercy, His protective presence.

The book of Exodus is so interested in the divine side of things, what *God did* for the Israelites, that it ignores completely points which are of interest to a modern reader. Who, for example, was the Pharao at the time of the Exodus, the journey out of Egypt? When did the liberation take place? Where was the crossing of the Sea effected? The Bible does not answer such questions, but modern scholars, armed with all the tools of historical and archaeological research, believe that they can.

The Exodus is generally dated to the last half of the 13th century B.C. during the reign of Pharao Rameses II. This father of 79 sons and 59 daughters seems to fit perfectly into the context of the Israelite adventures. Moses' rescue by the Egyptian princess situates the royal palace up north near the Delta where the Israelites lived. And that is where Rameses II had his palace. The name of the city built by the Israelites is called Rameses, a further allusion to that king who was an energetic, almost fanatical, builder. Other particulars, too, point to the 13th century period. Moses is spoken of as a contemporary of the first king of Moab, and archaeologists now claim that the Kingdom of Moab came into existence in the 13th century. A date of about 1250 B.C. for Moses and the Exodus seems best according to the evidence at hand.

So far as the crossing of the sea is concerned, it is usually located up above the main body of the Red Sea in the swampy land between that body of water and Lake Timsah to the north. In the Hebrew text the sea of the crossing is called *Yam Suph*, the *Reed Sea* (not Red Sea), thus suggesting some such swampy district.

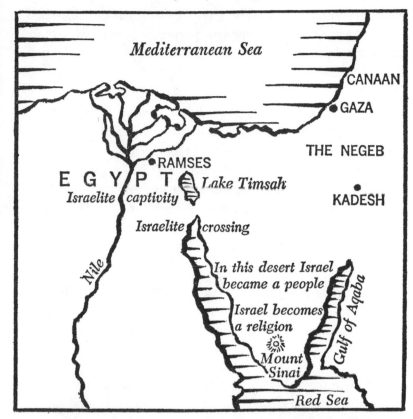

Since the 4th century A.D. the site of Mt. Sinai has been identified as Jebel Musa, the towering peak of an impressive range that lies at the southern end of the Sinai peninsula.

It is with particular reference to the events of the Exodus that Moses must be considered the Savior of the Israelites. This is the first of his two noble titles. When we speak of him leading the Israelites out of Egypt, we must understand the word Israelites as designating a disorganized mob. Most of it was composed of the descendants of Jacob-Israel, but there must have been others, too, individuals or groups, who took advantage of the opportunity to escape from slavery. Only in the desert did this group adopt a common life, a common purpose, a common law and leadership. In so doing the mob became a *people*.

People Become a Religion (*Read Exodus, chapters 19–20 for the covenant and the ten commandments: chapter 24 for the ratification of the covenant: chapter 25,1–27, 21 for the Ark of the Covenant and the Tent-Tabernacle: chapter 40 for the erection of the Ark and Tabernacle, and for the coming of the presence of God.*)

In the third month after their departure from the land of Egypt, on its first day, the Israelites came to the desert of Sinai. After the journey from Raphidim to the desert of Sinai, they pitched camp. While Israel was encamped here in front of the mountain, Moses went up the mountain to God (Exodus 19,1–3).

With these words begins the description of the second event of deep and eternal importance in the life of Moses. He has proved himself the Savior of the Israelite group which common life and purpose forged into a *people*; now he is to become the Mediator for the Israelite people with their God.

If you hearken to my voice and keep my covenant, you shall be my special possession, dearer to me than all other people, though all the earth is mine. You shall be to me a kingdom of priests, a holy nation (Exodus 19, 5–6).

Thus does God speak to Moses. The word covenant, as we have already seen with regard to Abraham, means agreement or pact. God initiates this one and determines its constitutive elements.

Basic to it is the notion that God has deigned to become a *Father* to this people which, in consequence, becomes His *son.* "Israel is my son, my first-born," says God in Exodus 4,23. To seal this agreement Moses takes the blood of young bulls, splashes half of it on the altar representing God, the other half on the people. By this symbolic act, God and the people become one family, blood relatives. Moses' words, familiar to Catholics because so like those of the consecration in the Mass, are:

This is the blood of the covenant which the Lord has made with you in accordance with all these words of his (Exodus 24,8).

As Father, God promises to protect His people; as son, the people promise to obey their divine Father. His will is manifest in the Ten Commandments, the basic law given to the Israelites. This law, or collection of laws, is elementary, the type of morality that could be appreciated by a rude people just escaping from long decades of slavery to a pagan nation. Each command is based on the most natural and obvious of virtues, justice, or respect for the rights of others. The first three concern the things which are due to God: unique adoration, respect, the offering of one day a week. The last seven concern the rights of others: the right which parents have to be honored by the children to whom they have given life, rights to one's property, to one's wife, to one's good name. Primitive and natural as these commands are, they are an excellent manifestation of God's concern with man's moral life. Upon such simple applications of justice, the noblest code of morality known to the world before the coming of Christ was built up over the centuries.

Other elements of this covenant are also observable. The most obvious are the *Ark of the Covenant* and the *Tent-Tabernacle.* The Ark was easily the most valuable possession of the Israelites. Most simple in style and composition, it was a chest (ark) some

3 feet long and 2 feet in breadth and height, made of setim wood, an incorruptible acacia. It was overlaid with gold, within and without, and contained within it the tablets of the Ten Commandments and, perhaps, some of the desert manna as well as Aaron's rod. But even more important than its contents was the throne placed on the level top of the Ark, a flat slab of pure gold of the same length and breadth as the Ark itself. This was decorated at the ends with a pair of carved cherubim. This slab was the "mercy seat" or "propitiatory," the place or instrument of propitiation, on which the blood of the victims was sprinkled by the High Priest on the Feast of the Atonement. The "Tabernacle" was the tent covering the Ark, and was constructed of a wooden framework with coverings of curtains and sheets. We are told that when Moses finished the construction of both Ark and Tabernacle-Tent and placed the one within the other, "the cloud covered the Meeting Tent, and the glory of the Lord filled the Dwelling" (Exodus 40,34). The Ark had a truly impressive twofold purpose: it contained the tablets of God's word, and, even more important, it was the dwelling place of Yahweh, the throne of His special presence on earth among His people.

When we consider all of these elements of the covenant—the Father and son relationship, the binding of God and people into one family, the common blood, the will of God expressed in the commandments and the intimate presence of God among His people—the thought must strike us that what the Israelites referred to as *covenant* we would call *religion*. The Old Covenant, or the Mosaic Covenant, means the Old or Mosaic Religion in our idiom. The elementary idea behind the word religion is a binding together of God and man. Surely the covenant which God formed with His people did precisely that. God and man were bound together as Father and son. The Father's will was expressed; the son promised obedience. And the Father dwelt with His first-born. The religion which Moses mediated to the Israelites was, therefore, a true religion in every respect.

There was another outstanding feature to this religion: sacrificial worship. The types of sacrifice were various, but a few general categories are evident from the earliest state of this religion. There was the *holocaust* in which the entire victim was consumed by fire on the altar: the *communion-sacrifice* which consumed part of the victim, with the rest being given to the priests and to the offerer who shared it with family and friends in a common meal: the sacrifice of *expiation* in which the sprinkling of blood was the most prominent element: the offerings of *vegetables* (wheaten flour, first fruits), of *incense* and of the *shewbread*. This latter consisted of twelve cakes of flour laid out in two lines on the table in the Tabernacle. At the end of the week they were eaten by the priests and then renewed. They were a symbol of the pledge between the twelve tribes and Yahweh.

These sacrifices had a very profound meaning for the Israelites. They were considered gifts to God in the sense of tributes paid to Him Who had a right to all things. The communion sacrifices added the notion of union. Just as contracts of olden times were sealed by a common meal, so the covenant, the religion between God and His family, was strengthened by a meal in which God, the priests, and the offerer's family and friends all shared. The sacrifices of expiation indicated the fundamental urge that all men have of the need of reparation for sins. The abuse of God's creatures by sin should be followed by the voluntary abstention from even some valid use of them.

With this added note of sacrifice, the elements of the Mosaic Religion stand complete. The world's history of salvation has begun a new phase in man's journey back to the God and the GOODNESS of God which man left at the entrance of sin into the world. Moses' role in mediating this religion to man is his greatest glory. He was both *savior* and *mediator*, and surely the latter function was far and away the more important.

One further point must be underlined with regard to Moses. Not only was he a savior and a mediator, he was also a *prophet*. A prophet is, quite simply, one who speaks for another, a spokesman. Moses was God's prophet because he spoke for God, relaying God's word to men. The book of Deuteronomy 18,15 contains an important promise made by Moses with regard to his prophetic function.

A prophet like me will the Lord, your God, raise up for you from among your own kinsmen; to him you shall listen.

This promise of Moses concerning the prophet like himself is one that the people remembered through subsequent centuries. In the later history of Israel there would be many prophets, each of them performing the spokesman-for-God function of Moses, each of them partial fulfillment of the promise of Deuteronomy 18,15. Yet the Israelites continued to expect an outstanding prophet, a new Moses, who would be the ultimate in God's messengers.

The Exodus from Egypt and the religious events atop Mount Sinai were the two central events in Israelite history that were never forgotten. They formed the basis of the people's common worship (liturgy) and prayer life, acting both as a memorial of things past and an assurance of present and future help. Through the liturgical presentation of these two events Israelites of all centuries could enter personally into the covenant struck between God and their ancestors. The Exodus, especially, was reenacted yearly in the life of every Israelite. Each year the Passover liturgy saw the individual families standing around the table as men ready for a journey, sandals on their feet, staffs in hand, garments tucked up, eating the paschal lamb with herbs of bitterness and unleavened bread. The renewal of this liturgy was an annual profession of faith in the mighty and loving God Who had brought His people out of bondage into the land He had promised to Abraham and his seed. The core of this liturgy is apparent in Exodus 12, 24–27:

You shall observe this as a perpetual ordinance for yourselves and your descendants. Thus, you must also observe this rite when you have entered the land which the Lord will give you as he promised. When your children ask you, 'What does this rite of yours mean?' you shall reply, 'This is the Passover sacrifice of the Lord, who passed over the houses of the Israelites in Egypt; when he struck down the Egyptians, he spared our houses.'

A similar profession of faith is found in the ritual for the offering of the first fruits.

The priest shall then receive the basket from you and shall set it in front of the altar of the Lord, your God. Then you shall declare before the Lord, your God, 'My father was a wandering Aramean who went down to Egypt with a small household and lived there as an alien. But there he became a nation great, strong and numerous. When the Egyptians maltreated and oppressed us, imposing hard labor upon us, we cried to the Lord, the God of our fathers, and he heard our cry and saw our affliction, our toil and our oppression. He brought us out of Egypt with his strong hand and outstretched arm, with terrifying power, with signs and wonders; and bringing us into this country, he gave us this land flowing with milk and honey (Deuteronomy 26, 4–9).

This passage can well be called the Israelite "Apostles' Creed," a veritable summation of what they knew of God and of their own religious character.

Solemn renewals of the Mount Sinai covenant were fairly frequent in the subsequent history of the people. When Josue finally succeeded in bringing the tribes into the Promised Land he performed a ceremony of renewal so that his followers who had not been alive at the stirring event of Mount Sinai might personally attest their acceptance of the religion which bound them to Yahweh. (See Josue, chapter 24.) Solomon's dedication of the temple as recorded in 3 Kings 8,54–61 is another example of such a solemn reenactment of the covenant. But the most ordinary way of keeping these divine acts before the minds of the people was by the daily praying of the psalms, so many of which hymn the praises of God Who freed the people from Egypt and united them to Himself as His first-born son. Psalms 110 (111), 77 (78) and 104 (105) are just a few of the many examples of such memorial prayers.

Now we can look back and see how the family of Abraham and Isaac and Jacob-Israel has grown numerous during the sojourn in Egypt; how the family has become a common people in the desert; how this people has become a religious body through the wondrous actions of God in the Sinai peninsula. Long years yet await it in the heat, cold, thirst and famine of the desert, but its character is now moulded. The years of discipline which follow, simply carry on the work of formation. These are years of training, training in obedience, training especially in trust in God's providence because the physical welfare of Moses and his followers depends totally upon God. These are years of faithful service, marred, unfortunately, by periods of infidelity. Moses himself loses confidence on occasions and, as a result, is denied the privilege of setting foot upon the Promised Land and of leading the people into it. The whole story is told in the books of Numbers and Deuteronomy which, together with Genesis, Exodus, and Leviticus are called the Pentateuch (the five books) of Moses. The final chapter of Deuteronomy presents us with the moving scene of Moses' last days. After the long years of desert

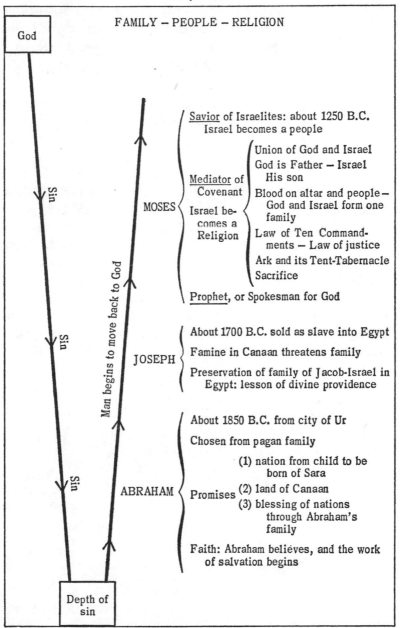

Chapter Two

FAMILY – PEOPLE – RELIGION

God

Sin

Sin

Sin

Depth of sin

Man begins to move back to God

MOSES

<u>Savior</u> of Israelites: about 1250 B.C. Israel becomes a people

<u>Mediator</u> of Covenant

Israel becomes a Religion

- Union of God and Israel
- God is Father – Israel His son
- Blood on altar and people – God and Israel form one family
- Law of Ten Commandments – Law of justice
- Ark and its Tent-Tabernacle
- Sacrifice

<u>Prophet</u>, or Spokesman for God

JOSEPH

- About 1700 B.C. sold as slave into Egypt
- Famine in Canaan threatens family
- Preservation of family of Jacob-Israel in Egypt: lesson of divine providence

ABRAHAM

- About 1850 B.C. from city of Ur
- Chosen from pagan family
- Promises
  - (1) nation from child to be born of Sara
  - (2) land of Canaan
  - (3) blessing of nations through Abraham's family
- Faith: Abraham beliéves, and the work of salvation begins

trial he and his people have arrived at a position just east of Canaan. There Moses ascends Mount Nebo in the heights of the country of Moab from which he can look westward across the Jordan River into the Promised Land.

The Lord then said to him, 'This is the land which I swore to Abraham, Isaac and Jacob that I would give to their descendants. I have let you feast your eyes upon it, but you shall not cross over.' So there, in the land of Moab, Moses, the servant of the Lord, died as the Lord had said; and he was buried in the ravine opposite Beth-Phogor in the land of Moab, but to this day no one knows the place of his burial. Moses was one hundred and twenty years old when he died, yet his eyes were undimmed and his vigor unabated. For thirty days the Israelites wept for Moses in the plains of Moab, till they had completed the period of grief and mourning for Moses . . . Since then no prophet has arisen in Israel like Moses, whom the Lord knew face to face. He had no equal in all the signs and wonders the Lord sent him to perform in the land of Egypt against Pharao and all his servants and against all his land, and for the might and the terrifying power that Moses exhibited in the sight of all Israel (Deuteronomy 34,4–12).

3

NATION AND KINGDOM

A Nation (*Read Josue, chapters 1–12 and 24*)

After Moses, the servant of the Lord, had died, the Lord said to Moses' aide Josue, son of Nun: 'My servant Moses is dead. So prepare to cross the Jordan here, with all the people, into the land which I will give the Israelites. As I promised Moses, I will deliver to you every place where you set foot' (Josue 1,1–13).

WITHOUT LAND AND COUNTRY of its own, a people is *not yet a nation.* So it was with the Israelites. At the death of Moses they were still nomads, a wandering people. It is the book of Josue which tells us of the conquest of Canaan and the evolution of Abraham's descendants into a nation.

Moses, as we have seen, was not to lead the people into Canaan. That duty fell upon the shoulders of his lieutenant, Josue, son of Nun, of the tribe of Ephraim, who had been consecrated successor to Moses in a formal ceremony before priest and community (Numbers 27,22–23). The first step in the conquest was the crossing of the Jordan River, the eastern boundary of the land of Canaan. Here something similar to the divinely arranged crossing of the Red Sea by Moses occurred. The water of the Jordan dried up as the Ark was carried into it. On the western side of the river, Canaanite territory, the Passover was celebrated and the

Ark installed in its Tent at Galgal where it remained for some five years.

The first encounter with the Canaanites took place at Jericho, close to the river crossing. Here, God again came to the aid of His people and the town was captured with a minimum of effort. God had entered once more into the Israelite adventures, convincing the people of His abiding presence among them and His continuous protection. It was this mental conviction of the people which helps to explain a series of happenings in the story of Josue which can be of scandalous nature to a modern reader of the book. On numerous occasions we read in Josue of the implementation of the *herem,* the complete slaughter of the inhabitants of the towns which the Israelites overcame. Such a practice was very common at that time. It was employed, and rejoiced in, by the Moabites and Ammonites who lived to the east of Canaan, and by the Assyrians who lived to the north-east a few centuries later. The Arab Holy Wars during the Christian era employed the same technique, and even the Crusaders befouled their swords in innocent blood. The modern expedient of total warfare is simply a more sophisticated version of the same type of destruction. (Think of Hiroshima and Nagasaki!) But the possible scandal of the book of Josue is that it affirms that the Israelite killings were commanded by God Himself.

Some students of this matter have argued that God has absolute power over life, and that He could exercise that power just as properly through *herems* as through auto accidents, floods, earthquakes, or avalanches. That may be.

However, it is also possible to interpret the descriptions of God commanding *herems* in a quite different fashion. The Hebrew people realized much better than we do that God is the basic cause of all things. No matter what happened, it was caused by God in some manner. Of this the Israelites were absolutely certain. They also saw clearly that these massacres had a number of

good effects. They punished the grossly immoral cults of the
Canaanites, gave the land to the twelve tribes, and reduced or
eliminated the dangerous attractions that Canaanite idolatries
extended to the Israelites. Consequently, the author of the book
of Josue dramatized this combination of the *herems'* good effects
and God's universal causality by saying that God commanded the
slaughters. Whatever God caused (and He caused everything),
as long as it had a good effect, God commanded. Such is the
author's reasoning, such his turn of phrase. This may well be the
most exact, and most consoling, explanation of this difficult
problem.

The conquest of Canaan was, in general, successful. Some
pockets of resistance held out for years, indeed for centuries, but
most of the Canaanite cities were conquered within a period,
roughly, of some fifty years. Besides the element of divine assistance, two other facts of strictly natural origin doomed the
Canaanites to defeat. One was their lack of unity. Josue 12,34,
mentions thirty-one individual kings in this small territory. In such
circumstances the Israelites didn't have to divide to conquer; the
Canaanites were already divided. A second natural occurrence
dooming the Canaanites was that during their period of resistance
to the Israelites who had attacked from the east, they were invaded from the western coast by the Philistines, sea people from
the islands near the mainland of Greece. The result of this two-
front attack was inevitable. The Canaanites were routed, and the
main body of survivors moved north into the territory called
Phoenicia where they eventually built up a remarkable maritime
empire. Two of their most important and best-known cities were
Tyre and Sidon.

As the Canaanites were routed or slaughtered, their land was
portioned out to the various Israelite tribes. Ruben, Gad, and half
the tribe of Manasse had already received territory on the

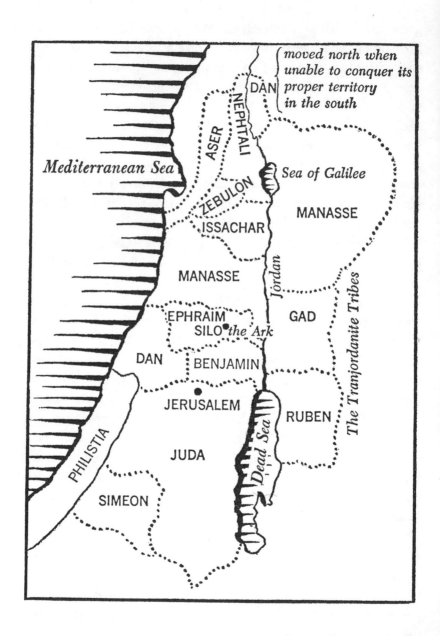

moved north when
unable to conquer its
proper territory
in the south

DAN

NEPHTALI

ASER

Mediterranean Sea

Sea of Galilee

ZEBULON

MANASSE

ISSACHAR

Jordan

MANASSE

The Tranjordanite Tribes

EPHRAIM

SILO •*the Ark*

GAD

DAN

BENJAMIN

• JERUSALEM

RUBEN

Dead Sea

JUDA

PHILISTIA

SIMEON

eastern side of the Jordan, the Transjordan. The others now received a tribal allotment. The boundaries of these territories cannot be determined with perfect accuracy, but the map gives a good idea of where the different tribes settled down. The Levites, as we have already noted, were not to receive any common territory, though they did obtain various cities from the different tribes.

Such were the tribal boundaries, such the nation, for a period of some two hundred years, *a nation without king, without capital, without parliament.* What united it was its dedication to Yahweh, its common religion. The external and visible sign of this religious unity was the Ark of the Covenant resting in its Tent in the city of Silo, in the territory of Ephraim (Josue 18,1).

The final incident of both historical and religious significance in the Josue story of Israel-become-nation is recounted in chapters eight and twenty-four. These accounts tell us of the impressive covenant renewal sponsored by Josue. The people pledged themselves to their God and to obedience to His law. The covenant struck between God and Moses was no static thing. New persons born into this nation and religion had to enter into the covenant in a personal manner, committing themselves to it just as firmly as had Moses and their forefathers in the desert.

As Israel received her land and became a nation, the second ancient promise made by God to Abraham was fulfilled. The first was the promise of a *numerous family* of descendants to rise from the yet unborn son of Abraham's aged and sterile wife, Sara. This promise was fulfilled in the birth of Isaac and the growth of the Israelites. The second was the promise of *the land.* This promise stands fulfilled at the end of the book of Josue. Yet unfulfilled is the mysterious saying about the blessing which would descend upon all the nations because of Abraham and his family.

Period of the Judges: (*Read Judges, chapters 1–16*)

This period covers some two hundred years following the invasion of Canaan by Josue's army. During it, as has already been mentioned, the nation was united by common family background and, especially, by its common religion symbolized and embodied in the Ark of the Covenant. The word *judge*, here, is somewhat of a misnomer, since the men so designated were not judges in our sense of the word. They were, rather, charismatic (divinely gifted) military leaders, somewhat like Joan of Arc, but without necessarily possessing Joan's sanctity. They were men whom God chose to lead the people during a time of military danger. And there were many such times, for Israel was bordered by enemies to the north and east, and had the most dangerous enemy of all, the Philistines, living inside of Canaan along the Plain of Sharon which forms the Mediterranean sea coast.

This period is one of scant importance for the history of salvation, except as a demonstration of how easily and often God's people fell away from His law and from their commitment to the covenant, and of how merciful and forgiving God was. These two centuries saw a repeated turning from God to the worship of idols. Not all the pagan Canaanites had been eradicated, still less had the influence of their pagan rites been eliminated. Israel time and again forsook her God to prostrate herself at the feet of the Canaanite Baal and Astarte, the god and goddess of fertility. Because of this, says the author of Judges, God punished them by powerful uprisings of their enemies.

But God was merciful, too, and raised military leaders, the judges, to rescue Israel once her time of punishment was finished. Twelve of these leaders are mentioned, and some of the tales of their exploits are of epic dimensions. There was the left-handed Aod of Benjamin who killed Eglon, king of Moab, with a two-edged sword a foot long (Judges 3,12–30). And Gedeon of Manasse who gradually diminished his army to emphasize the fact that his military strength rested, not in numbers, but in God's help. Then, with a tiny army he defeated his vastly superior enemy (Judges 6,1–8,28). And who can forget Samson of the tribe of Dan, Samson the sinner, "the colossus with feet of clay?" His daring adventures were directed against the Philistines, and, notwithstanding his sensual and brutish nature, it was he who protected the Israelites against those foes, always powerful because of the iron chariots and weapons which they possessed but Israel lacked (Judges 13,1–16,31).

Set in this period is the story of Ruth who lived "in the time of the judges." The beauty of the story stems from the widowed Ruth's tender love for Naomi, her mother-in-law. "But Ruth said, 'Do not ask me to abandon or forsake you! for wherever you go I will go, and wherever you lodge I will lodge; your people shall be my people and your God my God'" (Ruth 1,16). In the history of salvation, however, Ruth's importance comes from her child Obed: "He was the father of Jesse, the father of David" (4,17) who would be *the* king of Israel. Ruth was David's great-grandmother.

THE KINGDOM

Samuel and Saul (*Read 1st Book of Kings, also called 1st Book of Samuel*)

Samuel was born about 1060 B.C. to aged parents who had previously been childless. His birth was, consequently, an *Act of God* in the most literal sense of the words. As a small child he was brought to the sanctuary of the Ark of the Covenant in the town of Silo where, even at that tender age, he entered into the service of the Lord. Eli was the sanctuary priest of the time. He was a man of weak character, powerless to prevent his two sons from stealing the offerings made to God and from abusing the women who came as pilgrims to the shrine. So it happened that one dark night God called to the boy Samuel. "Speak, Lord," answered the child, "for thy servant hears." And the Lord spoke, spoke words that startled the ears of all that heard it. Disaster was foretold, the severe punishment of Eli and his sons. This was not long in coming. In the battle of Aphek (about 1050 B.C.) the two sons were killed as the Israelites retreated before the iron weapons of the Philistines. Even the Ark was seized as a prize of war. And Eli, when he heard this frightful news, fell backward from the chair on which he sat, and died.

For some twenty years following the death of Eli, Samuel was the guiding personality of the nation. He was, in fact, a judge, the last of the judges, and one who actually settled the cases proposed to him by his fellow citizens. Even more, much more, he was a *prophet,* a messenger of God who relayed the will of God to the people, and the prayers of the people to God. Samuel has been called the last of the judges and the first of the prophets. This is true if by "the first of the prophets" we mean the first of a long and continuous line of prophets who rose in succeeding generations. Before him, but widely separated in time, were both Abraham and Moses, God's eminent spokesmen. But with Samuel, century after century had its prophets and Samuel was the first of this long line.

The life of this prophet was not very happy or peaceful. The Ark had been captured by the Philistines and for some years afterwards remained in their possession, bringing misfortune into every town in which it was kept. This loss of the Ark surely saddened Samuel even more than it did his countrymen. Even worse, in losing the Ark, the Israelites also lost their faith in the abiding providence of God. The sanctuary at Silo lay in ruins;

the Ark was a captive. The Israelites looked for the explanation of their enemies' success and their own failure. The surrounding countries possessed human kings; they did not. Maybe that was what they needed, and so the Israelites demanded a king from Samuel. Up to this time their king, their only king, had been God Himself. Now, in their weakness, they considered the kingship of God insufficient. Their hopes turned from their King in heaven to the possible successes of a king on earth.

Samuel interpreted this demand for a king as a rejection of God, but he was unable to change the mind of the people. "No!" they shouted, "but we will have a king over us, that we also may be like all the nations, and that our king may govern us and go out before us and fight our battles . . . And the Lord said to Samuel, 'Hearken to their voice, and make them a king' " (I Kings, or 1 Samuel, 8,19–22).

The first king of Israel was Saul of the tribe of Benjamin. "There was not a man among the people of Israel more handsome than he; from his shoulders upwards he was taller than any of the people" (1 Kings, or 1 Samuel 9,2). He appears for the first time in a most humble fashion, trudging along afoot on the dusty road running north through the hill country of Ephraim in search of his father's lost she-asses. These he finds, with the help of the prophet Samuel. The episode comes to a climax when Samuel takes a vial of oil and with it anoints Saul as king of Israel.

Saul's first years as king were extremely successful. His important deeds were all military. Organizing and uniting the forces of Israel, he led them into battle against the Philistines whom he pushed back into their own territory along the western coastline of Palestine. Saul was indeed more warrior than king. His capital city of Gibea, a few miles north of Jerusalem, has been excavated. The modest size of its buildings during the reign of Saul tells us of a king untouched by those illusions of human grandeur which would be entertained by most of his successors.

Saul's story, however, ends in tragedy. Chosen by God to be His anointed representative, he fails to live up to the lofty responsibility of his office. He listens to the voice of the people rather than to Yahweh. The condemning words of Samuel in 1 Kings (or 1 Samuel) 15,22–23 designate the offense perfectly:

Has the Lord as great delight in burnt offerings and sacrifices, as in obeying the voice of the Lord? Behold, to obey is better than sacrifice, and to hearken than the fat of rams. For rebellion is as the sin of divination, and stubbornness is as iniquity and idolatry. Because you have rejected the word of the Lord, he has also rejected you from being king.

After this rejection Saul goes from bad to worse, from disobedience to the murder of the priests of Nob, from jealousy to the madness of a persecution complex, spending time and strength in a futile pursuit of David while Israel's real enemy, the Philistines, score military victories. He dies by his own hand (1 Kings 31,4), or by that of the Amelicite (2 Kings 1,10); not even the author of the book is certain which of these two similar descriptions is the more exact. Such was the sad life, such the tragic end of a man who would not be king in accordance with God's will. His kingship was limited to himself, his descendants were not to inherit the throne. Yet through Saul the nation had become a kingdom.

King David (*Read 2 Kings, also called 2 Samuel*)

David is first presented to us in connection with the fall of Saul from God's favor. The prophet Samuel is sent to Bethlehem to anoint the man who will replace Saul. The man is found, David, the youngest son of Jesse, the son who "was ruddy, and had beautiful eyes, and was handsome." He sounds like the All-

Israelite boy, and, indeed, he must have been. His lyre soothes the ever deepening distemper and melancholy of King Saul. His sling dispatches the smooth stone that fells Goliath, the giant Philistine, and wins the day for the Israelite army. David's accuracy with sling and stone reminds us of the bold hyperbole of the book of Judges 20,16. We read there of the Benjaminites (as was David) who assembled for battle. "Included in this total," says the enthusiastic author, "were seven hundred picked men who were left-handed, every one of them able to sling a stone at a hair without missing." David must have been no less accurate.

David's relationship to King Saul and his royal family was complicated by the jealousy which the King felt for him. David, on his part, respected Saul almost to an extreme. On at least one occasion (1 Kings 24,1–22; 26,1–25) David could easily have killed Saul who was at that very moment trying to put him to death. David rejected the opportunity, ever respectful to the man whom the Lord had anointed.

The friendship which grew up between David and Jonathan, son of Saul, has become proverbial. We are told that "the soul of Jonathan was knit to the soul of David, and Jonathan loved him as his own soul." And Saul's daughter Michal became David's wife. Strange story! Saul, at the very edge of madness, seeks to kill David, husband of his daughter and closest friend of his son. Finally, when both Saul and Jonathan are killed by the Philistines, David sings an elegy, a song of sorrow, whose deeply felt emotion can be clearly sensed as we read it now, some 3000 years later.

Thy glory, O Israel, is slain upon thy high places! How are the mighty fallen! . . . Ye mountains of Gilboa, let there be no dew nor rain upon you . . . for there was the shield of the mighty defiled, the shield of Saul . . . Saul and Jonathan, beloved and lovely! In life and death they were not divided; they were swifter than eagles, they were stronger than lions . . . How are the mighty fallen in the midst of battle! Jonathan lies slain upon thy high places. I am distressed for you, my brother Jonathan; very pleasant have you been to me; your love to me was wonderful, passing the love of women. How are the mighty fallen, and the weapons of war perished (2 Kings 1,19–27).

The death of Saul was followed by a short civil war to choose his successor. The North favored Ishbaal, surviving son of Saul, while the South favored David, setting him up as king in the city of Hebron. The war was short-lived, however, and David was soon accepted as king of all Israel. This North-South rivalry was still a danger lurking close to the surface, so David chose as his capital a city which he had just conquered; one, consequently, which had no past connection with either geographical section. This city was, of course, Jerusalem, close to the North-South boundary. Here David ruled for about forty years. This allows us to note one of the hinge dates, and an easy one to remember, for the Old Testament. In the year 1000 B.C. David was king in Jerusalem. To make the city more than a simple political center David brought to it the Ark of the Covenant, now returned from the Philistines. With this wise move David made Jerusalem the religious center of Palestine, the site of God's presence, and the focal point of Israelite worship.

The story of David's life remains incomplete without the account of his grave sin, and of the punishment which followed from it. David's passionate attachment to Bethsheba, wife of Uria, led to his moral downfall. Adultery is compounded with murder as David schemes to have Uria placed helpless in the most dangerous part of the battle. The scheme works: Uria is killed and Bethsheba enters David's palace as queen. And in her footsteps comes the courageous figure of Nathan, prophet of the Lord, a successor to Samuel who is now dead. He faces up to this mighty king, reproves him for his sins and predicts the grave punishments which those sins will draw from the hand of God. David's response is admirable in its simplicity: "I have sinned against the Lord." David follows this with a fast of seven days and seven nights.

The years that followed were difficult ones for David. If ever a man suffered for his one abysmal period of sinful weakness, David was that man. Jonathan, his other soul, was dead. Michal, his first wife, turned into a shrew. Absolom, one of his best loved sons, led an almost successful revolution to topple his father's throne. And yet when this rebellious son was killed, David was brokenhearted. "O my son Absolom," he cried, "my son, my son Absolom! Would I had died instead of you, O Absolom, my son, my son" (2 Kings 18,33).

What an extraordinary man, this David! Shepherd boy, warrior-hero, resourceful lover, bandit chieftain, poet, king, sinner, penitent, indulgent father, faithful friend, founder of an eternal dynasty! Down through the centuries he remained *the* king of Israel, the scale for the measure of all subsequent kings.

David and the Story of Salvation (*Reread 2 Kings, chapter seven*)

If we have spent so much time detailing the life history of David, it has been to place a necessary emphasis upon this man who had so important a role in the story of salvation. Until the appearance of David, this story has seen God elect one man, Abraham, and has seen this one man produce a child (Isaac) whose descendants grow into a family, a people, a nation, a kingdom. This has meant that successively the hope of salvation resided in one man, in his family, his people, his nation, his kingdom. That is the picture when David is anointed king. However, during his reign something happened which gave a new direction to the hope of salvation. In 2 Kings, chapter seven, we read that when David had finished building his palace he was ashamed to think that the Ark, the site of God's dwelling, was protected by nothing more sumptuous than the Tent-Tabernacle. He began to plan a Temple, a magnificent house for the Lord. But that same night the word of the Lord came to the prophet Nathan. Its message was profound, one which impressed itself deeply on the Israelite mind. Instead of David building a house for the Lord, the Lord would build a *house for David,* i.e., a dynasty. Let us look at the words of the text:

Moreover the Lord declares to you that the Lord will make you a house. When your days are fulfilled and you lie down with your fathers, I will raise up your son after you, who shall come forth from your body, and I will establish his kingdom. He shall build a house for my name, and *I will establish the throne of his kingdom for ever. I will be his father, and he shall be my son.* When he commits iniquity, I will chasten him with the rod of men, with the stripes of the sons of men; but I will not take my steadfast love from him, as I took it from Saul, whom I put away from before you. And *your house and your kingdom shall be made sure for ever before me; your throne shall be established for ever* (2 Kings, or 2 Samuel, 7,11–16).

This is called the prophecy of Nathan, and it is referred to often in other books of the Old Testament, especially in the psalms. Psalm 88 (89), for example, speaks almost entirely of this agreement, of this covenant, between God and David. Psalm 2 is another psalm hymning the message of Nathan. In this latter psalm we are told that David's kingdom will be universal, not merely in time (as in 2 Kings 7), but also in extent.

Nathan's message to David, therefore, tells him that he and his descendants have entered in a special way into the plans of God. His kingdom will be an eternal one, and in a way and at a time unknown to him, universal. Not only that, but the kings themselves, the successors to David, will be the *sons of God*. This title was, we remember, the proud title of all the Israelites. Now it belongs, in a particular manner, to the kings. This means that the Davidic kings enter into the Mosaic covenant, the Mosaic religion, in a unique fashion. The king now stands as mediator. He, as special son of God, will (or should) represent God to the people; he will also represent the people before God. Israel will see in the king the visible sign of God's protection, and a pledge of God's fidelity to the mighty promise He has made. The birth of every Davidic prince, the consecration of every Davidic king in future years will be an occasion of rejoicing, for that prince or that king stands close to God and may perhaps be the mysterious king who will possess the kingdom both universal in extent and eternal in duration. The people were in this way being prepared for the coming of some extraordinary descendant of David who would have a crucial role to play in the history of salvation—a royal Messia.

The description of David's transfer of the Ark to Jerusalem and of the worship he encouraged there gives us a further view of his sacred priestly character as king. Enroute to Jerusalem "David and all the house of Israel were making merry before the Lord with all their might, with songs and lyres and harps and tambourines and castanets and cymbals" (2 Kings 6,5). After the Ark was installed in the Tent-Tabernacle, David supervised the form of prayer worship which would glorify God in that holy place.

And when David had finished offering the burnt offerings and the peace offerings, he blessed the people in the name of the Lord, and distributed to all Israel, both men and women, to each a loaf of bread, a portion of meat, and a cake of raisins. Moreover he appointed certain of the Levites as ministers before the ark of the Lord, to invoke, to thank, and to praise the Lord, the God of Israel . . . So David left

Asaph and his brethren there before the ark of the covenant of the Lord to minister continually before the ark as each day required . . . And he left Zadok the priest and his brethren the priests before the tabernacle of the Lord in the high place that was Gibeon, to offer burnt offerings to the Lord upon the altar of burnt offering continually morning and evening . . . Heman and Jeduthun had trumpets and cymbals for the music and instruments for sacred song (1 Chronicles, also called Parilopomenon, 16,2–42).

With David, therefore, God's plan of salvation takes another significant step forward. As Abraham was the *Father* of all Israelites and the one person with whom God initiated the plan, as Moses was the *Mediator* through whom God bound His people to Himself in a true covenant-religion, so David was the *King* whom God chose to found a kingdom which would one day be both eternal and universal and in which salvation would finally be found. From this time on the hopes of Israel and, indeed, the hopes of the world were directed toward the Davidic dynasty, toward the king reigning at that moment, and toward the great King who was to come in the future.

One final religious act of David must be mentioned. It consisted in the purchase of the threshing floor of Araunah in Jerusalem in order to build an altar at that spot. And, though David himself was not to build the temple, when it was built by his son Solomon it was built on this threshing floor. David died around 965 B.C., shortly after he had appointed Solomon as his successor.

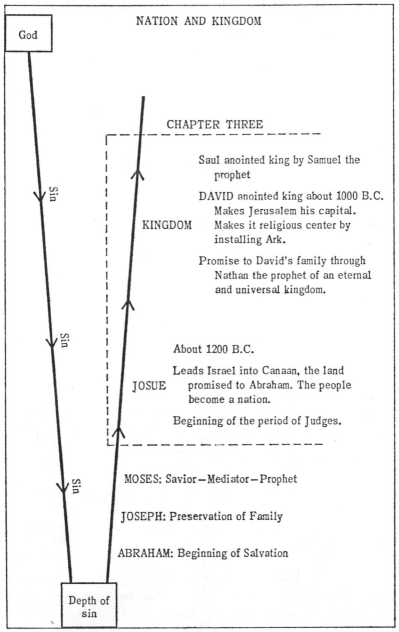

NATION AND KINGDOM

God

CHAPTER THREE

Sin

Saul anointed king by Samuel the
prophet

DAVID anointed king about 1000 B.C.
Makes Jerusalem his capital.
KINGDOM   Makes it religious center by
installing Ark.

Promise to David's family through
Nathan the prophet of an eternal
and universal kingdom.

Sin

About 1200 B.C.

Leads Israel into Canaan, the land
JOSUE   promised to Abraham. The people
become a nation.

Beginning of the period of Judges.

Sin

MOSES: Savior — Mediator — Prophet

JOSEPH: Preservation of Family

ABRAHAM: Beginning of Salvation

Depth of
sin

59

4

DIVISION OF THE KINGDOM— PRE-EXILIC PROPHETS

DIVISION OF THE KINGDOM

Solomon (*Read 3 Kings, chapters 1–11*)

SOLOMON, SON OF BETHSHEBA, was selected as king by David's deathbed decision in his favor over the claim of his older brother Adonija. Solomon began where David left off. His reign is proverbial for its grandeur and luxury. Clever in the ways of the world, he entered into the blooming field of international commerce and brought wealth into Jerusalem. Hundreds of war chariots were acquired, and thousands of horses. The remains of their stalls at the town of Megiddo have been brought to light by modern excavations and prove that the description given in 3 Kings 10,26 was no patriotic exaggeration.

And Solomon gathered together chariots and twelve thousand horsemen; he had fourteen hundred chariots and twelve thousand horsemen, whom he stationed in the chariot cities and with the king in Jerusalem.

His household provision for one day was "thirty measures of fine flour, and sixty measures of meal, ten fat oxen, and twenty pasture-fed cattle, a hundred sheep, besides hares, gazelles, roebucks, and fatted fowl" (3 Kings 4,22–23). We read that when the Queen of Sheba had seen "the food of his table, the seating of his officials, and the attendance of his servants, their clothing, his cupbearers, and his burnt offerings which he offered at the house of the Lord," she was overcome with amazement. His was the luxury of the Oriental court of old, and a far cry from the simplicity of Saul's capital, to say nothing of the utter poverty of the desert years of Moses and the people of the Exodus. Behind all this luxury lies a sad story of exorbitant taxes levied, tribe by tribe, on the common people. The eternal story of the rich becoming richer and the poor poorer was a daily reality during the lifetime of this high-living king.

Notwithstanding Solomon's corrupted interest in the good soft things of this world, he did make a contribution to the story of salvation and to the development of the Mosaic religion in which salvation was lodged. For a period of some seven years (about 960–953 B.C.) his energies were devoted to the building of a temple for the Lord on the threshing floor of Araunah previously purchased by his father, David. The best possible material was obtained: towering cedar trees from the Lebanon county to the north. The king of that territory, Hiram of Phoenicia, sent his finest artisans to help in the actual construction of the building. It was very simple in form, rectangular, small by modern standards, some 11 yards wide and 40 yards long. It was divided into three main sections: a vestibule (*Ulam*), a nave (*Hekal*), and the inner sanctuary itself (*Debir*), the Holy of Holies. Into the darkness of the Holy of Holies was placed the Ark of the Covenant. Once it was enclosed in that sanctuary and the cloud of the divine presence overshadowed it, the Ark in the Holy of Holies was the holiest object in the holiest spot in the world. Only the High Priest was allowed to enter into the sacred darkness, and that, just once a year on the solemn feast of Expiation.

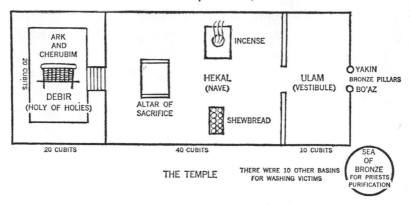

THE TEMPLE   THERE WERE 10 OTHER BASINS FOR WASHING VICTIMS

The liturgical worship surrounding the Ark which existed during David's reign was embellished. The Bible speaks of

all the Levitical singers, Asaph, Heman, and Jeduthun, their sons and kinsmen, arrayed in fine linen, with cymbals, harps, and lyres (who) stood east of the altar with a hundred and twenty priests who were trumpeters; and it was the duty of the trumpeters and singers to make themselves heard in unison in praise and thanksgiving to the Lord (2 Chronicles 5,12–13).

In such fashion did the externals of the Mosaic religion develop, externals which could (as is the danger in every religion) develop into a mere formalism, but which were meant to evince the desire of both king and people to offer to God the beauty of music and ceremony. The sacred character of Solomon, Davidic king and son of God, stands out plainly in the text which describes the dedication of the Temple. There we read that

as Solomon finished offering all this prayer and supplication to the Lord, he arose from before the altar of the Lord, where he had knelt with hands outstretched toward heaven; and he stood, and blessed all the assembly of Israel with a loud voice . . . The same day the king consecrated the middle of the court that was before the house of the

Lord; for there he offered the burnt offering and the cereal offering and the fat pieces of the peace offering . . . (3 Kings 8,54–55. 64).

In this scene Solomon acts more as priest than as king, or, better still, as priestly king occupying the privileged position between God and man that had been given to the Davidic kings by the prophecy of Nathan. The people must have wondered on an occasion like this whether Solomon himself might possibly be the kingly son of God to whom was promised a kingdom both eternal and universal.

Solomon also influenced the development of the Mosaic religion by his wisdom utterances and wisdom writings. The biblical tradition is very strong in insisting upon the deep wisdom of this man, and on the proverbs he uttered.

For he was wiser than all other men, wiser than Ethan the Ezrahite, and Heman, Calcol, and Darda, the sons of Mahol; and his fame was in all the nations round about. He also uttered three thousand proverbs; and his songs were a thousand and five (3 Kings, 4,31–32).

Many of these, surely, were handed down through the following centuries and have come to us in the canonical proverbs and psalms.

And yet this kingly son of God, this man of wisdom and of peace, ended up as a tragic religious figure, shamed and humiliated by his unchecked sensuality. His wives and concubines were counted in the scores, in the hundreds. Many of these were pagan women, and they brought with them as their religious dowry the worship of their pagan gods. Solomon's passive acceptance of such practices was the beginning of his sin. At its conclusion he was actually sharing in the worship of these false gods.

Now King Solomon loved many foreign women: the daughter of Pharao and Moabite, Ammonite, Edomite, Sidonian, and Hittite women . . . Solomon clung to these in love. He had seven hundred wives, princesses, and three hundred concubines; and his wives turned away his heart. For when Solomon was old his wives turned away his heart after other gods; and his heart was not wholly true to the Lord his God, as was the heart of David his father. For Solomon went after Ashtoreth the goddess of the Sidonians, and after Milcom the abomination of the Ammonites . . . Then Solomon built a high place for Chemosh the abomination of Moab, and for Molech the abomination of the Ammonites, on the mountain east of Jerusalem. And so he did for all his foreign wives, who burned incense and sacrificed to their gods (3 Kings 11,1–8).

God is not mocked, not even by his kingly son, and the divine punishment would not be long in appearing. Solomon's mighty kingdom of luxury barely outlasted his death:

'Since you have not kept my covenant and my statutes,' said the Lord to Solomon, 'I will surely tear the kingdom from you. . . . Yet for the sake of David your father I will not do it in your days, but I will tear it out of the hand of your son. However I will not tear away all the kingdom; but I will give one tribe to your son, for the sake of Jerusalem which I have chosen' (3 Kings 11,11–13).

And so Solomon died, old and corrupt, his wealthy and sinful kingdom poised on the brink of destruction.

The Schism (*Read 3 Kings 12,1–33*)

The destruction of the unity of Solomon's kingdom occurred shortly after his death about 932 B.C. His son and successor was Roboam, a young man with little of the proverbial wisdom of his father. It was at the northern town of Shechem, sacred to the memory of the patriarchs, that a financial question, checked only with difficulty during the lifetime of Solomon, burst to the surface. The question concerned the taxes and forced labor to which Solomon had bound the tribes in order to provide finances and workmen for his grandiose building projects.

With Roboam's accession hopes ran high for a more lenient administration and in particular, for a reduction in taxes. Beneath this desire for reform ran a deeper current, the traditional jealousy between north and south. This jealousy which had lain dormant during the grand years of David's reign, and had begun to stir again during the years of Solomon, was now clearly evident as Roboam arrived at Shechem for his consecration ceremony. There is some evidence that the onerous taxes of Solomon had not been imposed on the southern tribe of Juda. If this was true, then the northern tribes had carried the entire burden of financing Solomon's projects. The northern tribes now demanded a reduction in taxes of the youthful Roboam. Roboam proved himself a man of little or no political acumen, a man insensitive to the needs of the time and the temper of the people. Instead of a cut in taxes, he promised an increase. That did it. Led by the commoner Jeroboam, a former servant of Solomon, an Ephraimite (a northerner, consequently), the north revolted against the south and seceded from it. To the cry of:

> What portion have we in David?
> We have no inheritance in the son of Jesse.
> To your tents, O Israel!
> Look now to your own house, David (3 Kings 12,16)

the northern tribes broke from the Union. Roboam was left king of only a fraction of the kingdom of his father and grandfather, retaining control over the one tribe of Juda, and some members of the tribes of Benjamin and Simeon. The political work of Saul and David and Solomon was destroyed, and the Israelites were never again to know the united kingdom of all twelve tribes as it existed in the days of her first three kings.

One of the first, and most ominous, moves that the upstart king Jeroboam made in his northern kingdom (generally called *Israel* in distinction to the southern kingdom of *Juda*) was to counteract the religious popularity of Jerusalem, capital of the southern kingdom. He realized that the presence there of the Temple and Ark would exert a continuous attraction to the northern tribes to reunite with the south. Consequently, he constructed sanctuaries of his own, one at Dan in the northern extreme of his territory, the other at Bethel. This latter was not far from Jerusalem, and Jeroboam hoped that any pilgrims from his kingdom enroute to the Temple and Ark in Jerusalem could be induced to stop off at Bethel instead. At both Dan and Bethel he erected calves of gold (wooden statues, surely, encased in gold). This was not an out-and-out case of idolatry by any means. The calves were undoubtedly intended to represent the throne of Yahweh and to symbolize His power. But it proved impossible to retain this orthodox meaning, for the calf was also the symbol of the infamous Canaanite god Baal, the god of fertility. It would not be long before many of the Israelites would be bowing down before the golden calves not as symbolic representations of the throne of the invisible God of Israel, but as the visible sign of the fertility god. Jeroboam had initiated a most dangerous religious practice. By it he was successful in keeping his people from their pilgrimages to Jerusalem, but by it, also, he laid the seed for the future apostasy of Israel from her true God. This apostasy, however, would not be unopposed. Into the history of both Israel to the north and Juda to the south would step *the prophets of God* with their demands for conversion and their message of deep and abiding spirituality.

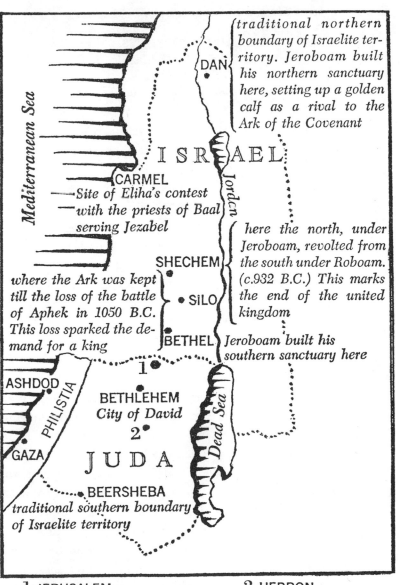

traditional northern boundary of Israelite territory. Jeroboam built his northern sanctuary here, setting up a golden calf as a rival to the Ark of the Covenant

Mediterranean Sea

I S R A E L

Jordan

DAN

CARMEL
—Site of Eliha's contest
—with the priests of Baal
serving Jezabel

here the north, under Jeroboam, revolted from the south under Roboam. (c.932 B.C.) This marks the end of the united kingdom

SHECHEM

where the Ark was kept till the loss of the battle of Aphek in 1050 B.C. This loss sparked the demand for a king

• SILO

BETHEL

Jeroboam built his southern sanctuary here

1 •

ASHDOD

PHILISTIA

•
BETHLEHEM
City of David

Dead Sea

2 •

GAZA

J U D A

•BEERSHEBA
traditional southern boundary of Israelite territory

1 JERUSALEM
capital of the southern kingdom of Juda and religious center of the Israelite world with the Ark of the Covenant

2 HEBRON
David king here. for seven years

PRE-EXILIC PROPHETS
ISRAELITE PROPHETISM

Most often the word *prophet* brings to mind the idea of a fore-teller of a distant future, a man with the type of long-range vision that would soon send every racetrack bookie to the poorhouse. This is, unfortunately, to confuse the office of the prophets. True, on rather rare occasions, they did foretell future happenings, usually in a vague and mysterious manner, but their main duty was to deliver a very clear and timely moral message from God to the king and people. They were God's spokesmen, His messengers, delivering God's demands for repentance and conversion to the people of their own day. Their message was meant for their own times, but its truth and importance remain valid today.

Moses was a prophet. Indeed, he was the greatest of God's messengers before the Christian era. But the *age* of the prophets, a period of some nine hundred years from about 1050 B.C. to 150 B.C. really begins with Samuel and the rise of the Israelite monarchy. Prophetism and monarchy sprang up almost together, and there was a close relationship between the two for centuries due to the fact that one of the main duties of the prophet was to advise and correct the king. This was a thankless task, since most of the kings of both the northern (Israel) and southern (Juda) kingdoms were far from being God-fearing men who welcomed the message of God. The phrase "reward of a prophet" had an ominous tone from the very beginning of prophetic history, for the prophets often suffered severely from their mission. They were beaten, imprisoned, insulted, put into stocks, sunk deep into muddy cisterns—but the only thing that silenced them was death, not infrequently by violence. We have already seen Samuel bring God's message of rejection to King Saul, and the courageous Nathan reprove David to his face for his murderous affair with Bethsheba. These confrontations were typical of the prophets' relationship with subsequent kings.

Not that the prophets' activity was limited to the kings. Others, too, felt the force of the divine message. The prophetic voice (and it was loud and clear) spoke out against the priests who betrayed their sacred trust by greed and idolatry, against the rich who ground the poor into destitution, and against the poor themselves who, like sheep following wayward shepherds, wandered into a life of aimless depravity. King, priests, nobles, rich, poor; to all these the prophets spoke. The intense spirituality of their teaching made an immense contribution to the religion of Moses and was yet another advance toward the period of salvation in which men would be saved by worshipping God in spirit and in truth.

Before treating of some of the more important of the pre-exilic prophets it might be well to give a rapid summation of their teaching in general. Their oracles and sermons centered on the following points:

Interior Spirituality. One of the truly inspiring teachings of the prophets (one as necessary for us today as it was for the Hebrew audiences to which it was first delivered) is that which insists on a true religion of the heart, one based on love of God and obedience to Him During the troubled times of the prophets, Israel's trust in the absolute and unfailing value of external ceremonies was shocking. Morally unwilling to serve God by the daily worship of obedience to His will, she quieted her conscience by multiplying altars and sacrifices. These she tragically presumed would call down God's mercy. A period of dry rot formalism had set in. Typical of the prophet's rejection of the pseudo-religion of external observances is that of Jeremia.

Thus says the Lord of hosts, the God of Israel: Reform your ways and your deeds, so that I may remain with you in this place. Put not your trust in the deceitful words; 'This is the temple of the Lord! The temple of the Lord! The temple of the Lord! Only if you thoroughly reform your ways and your deeds; if each of you deals justly with his neighbor; if you no longer oppress the resident alien, the orphan, and the widow; if you no longer shed innocent blood in this place, or follow strange gods to your own harm, will I remain with you in this place, in the land which I gave your fathers long ago and forever (Jeremia 7,3–7).

Unique Worship of the True God. The prophets railed constantly against the idolatry of their age. "I, the Lord, am your God . . . You shall not have other gods besides me" was the most necessary commandment of the period. Even such rarely good kings as Ezechia and Josia had only limited success in their campaigns to wipe out the idolatry of the times. Many Israelites offered up their children in fiery oblations to the pagan god Moloch. The body-like statue of this god was actually a huge furnace. Down its elevated arms, through its open chest, and into its flaming interior were rolled the innocent victims of pagan worship. Jeremia was to say that Juda's clothing was stained with "the life-blood of the innocent" (Jeremia 2,34).

The cult of Baal and the "queen of heaven" was equally revolting and even more extensive. Its basis was the yearly cycle of nature. Since nature seemed to die under the cruel summer sun and revive with the late autumn rains, a myth was invented to explain this pattern of the seasons. According to the myth, Baal, the fertility god, died in the dry season and was brought back to life in the autumn by his consort, "the queen of heaven." Their love-making produced the fertility of nature after the rains. Those convinced of the myth made it into a cult by imitating the love-making of the god and goddess, thus hoping to draw down on themselves the blessing of nature's productivity. Through such an imitative cult the people purposed to draw close to their amorous god and goddess and to insure the fertility of womb and field. This cult abounded in cult prostitutes and licentious fertility rites. These were truly the bane of religious life in the Israelite kingdoms. The prophets refer to them constantly, but without observable effect upon their listeners. They plead with the people, threaten them, cry over them, beg them to return and be faithful to the one and only God, to adore Him, the real Lord of nature, by complete obedience to His will.

Social Justice. This is another prophetic theme of modern application. The luxury of the palaces and grand mansions was built on injustice to the worker and on bribery of the judges in their open courts at the city gates. The merchants of the times stooped to the lowest forms of theft, weighing their produce on inaccurate scales (not unknown to our own age), thus sending their customers off with less than they paid for. The poor, the miserable, the dispossessed, said the prophets, were of particular importance in the sight of God. Woe to those who failed to treat them as *God's poor,* as *God's dispossessed.* This theme, so common to the prophets, was especially dear to Amos, the "prophet of man's duty to his fellow man."

> Thus says the Lord:
>   For three crimes of Israel, and for four,
>   I will not revoke my word;
> Because they sell the just man for silver,
>   and the poor man for a pair of sandals.
> They trample the heads of the weak
>   into the dust of the earth,
> and force the lowly out of the way . . . (Amos 2,6–7).

> Woe to those who turn judgment to wormwood
>   and cast justice to the ground!
> Therefore, because you have trampled upon the weak
>   and exacted of them levies of grain,

Though you have built houses of hewn stone,
   you shall not live in them!
Though you have planted choice vineyards,
   you shall not drink their wine.
Yes I know how many are your crimes,
   how grievous your sins:
Oppressing the just, accepting bribes,
   repelling the needy at the gate . . . (Amos 5,7–12).

Hear this, you who trample upon the needy
   and destroy the poor of the Land!
'When will the New Moon be over,' you ask,
   'that we may sell our grain,
   and the Sabbath, that we may display the wheat?
We will diminish the epha,
   add to the shekel,
   and fix our scales for cheating!
We will buy the lowly man for silver,
   and the poor man for a pair of sandals;
   even the refuse of the wheat we will sell!' (Amos 8,4–6).

This prophetic approach to the question of justice to the poor was a pre-Christian proclamation of the beatitudes. A cry for justice and mercy, it was, at the same time, an exaltation of the poor to the level of privilege in the sight and love of God.

Interior spirituality, worship of the true God only, justice toward the poor: these were the main themes of God's prophets. The kings, the priests, the nobles, the rich, the people as a whole: these constituted their audience. But what about the individual prophets themselves? Who were they and what kind of men were they? Representative of them, and most important for the part they played in this fight against the *powerful kingdom of sin,* were Elia, Elisha, Amos, Osee, Isaia, Michea, and Jeremia.

INDIVIDUAL PRE-EXILIC PROPHETS

Elia and Elisha (*Read 3 Kings 16,23—4 Kings 13,21*)

The ministry of these two miracle-working prophets revolved around the kingship of Ahab, King of Israel about the year 870 B.C. It was Ahab's father, King Omri, who moved the capital of the northern kingdom to the city of Samaria. We know from non-biblical sources that the period of Omri was one of worldly prestige, of wealth and luxury. He made a valuable alliance with the neighboring merchant country of Phoenicia, sealing the bond by the marriage of his son Ahab to Jezebel, the Phoenician princess. But our inspired author is not the least bit interested in Omri's material successes. His kingship is judged tersely and sadly by reference to his spiritual failure.

Omri did what was evil in the sight of the Lord, and did more evil than all who were before him. For he walked in all the way of Jeroboam . . . and in the sins which he made Israel to sin, provoking the Lord, the God of Israel, to anger by their idols (3 Kings 16,25–26).

Jezebel, Ahab's pagan wife, was a stronger character than her husband. Between her and the prophet *Elia* was a lifelong enmity, for she had brought with her from Phoenicia the worship of her god Baal. She set up altars to him in Samaria and installed priests there for his licentious worship. She put to death the prophets of the Lord, Elia alone escaping her murderous hand. In Samaria, therefore, the kingdom of sin had taken over with a vengeance.

Chapter eighteen of the Third Book of Kings gives a vivid description of the famous contest atop Mount Carmel between Jezebel's priests of Baal and the lonely figure of Elia. This is a face to face encounter, a duel, between the power of Baal and that of Yahweh. Both sides set out their animal victims. The priests of Baal pray all morning for fire to come down to consume their victims. Nothing happens. Urged on mockingly by Elia, they continue their prayers throughout the afternoon. "Cry aloud," taunted Elia, "for he is a god; either he is musing, or he has gone aside, or he is on a journey, or perhaps he is asleep and must be awakened" (verse 27). Still nothing happens. Then Elia floods his victim in water, prays, and fire comes down to consume the animal. The contest ends with the priests of Baal being put to death.

But Jezebel lived on, and Elia's life remained in continual danger. He had already objected to the *idolatry* flourishing in Ahab's kingdom. His next prophetic function was to object to the king concerning a vile bit of *social injustice* in which the king and queen were involved. It concerned the vineyard of Naboth in the city of Jezreel. This vineyard was next to the king's property and was strongly desired by him. But Naboth refused to sell since the land was an inheritance from his ancestors. The king was sad, despondent. But Jezebel's reaction was different. She simply had Naboth brought to trial on a trumped up charge that he had cursed both God and king. The verdict was "Guilty." Naboth was stoned to death, and the king got the vineyard. Then the prophet appeared on the scene.

Then the word of the Lord came to Elia . . . saying, 'Arise, go down to meet Ahab king of Israel, who is in Samaria: behold, he is in the vineyard of Naboth, where he has gone to take possession. And you shall say to him, 'Thus says the Lord, Have you killed and also taken possession?' And you shall say to him, 'Thus says the Lord: In the place where the dogs licked up the blood of Naboth shall dogs lick your own blood.' . . . And of Jezebel the Lord also said, 'The dogs shall eat Jezebel within the bounds of Jezreel' (3 Kings 21,17–19. 23).

These two instances of Elia's warfare against idolatry and social injustice are examples of the mission of all Israelite prophets. They carried the message of God, sparking the consciences of the evildoers, picturing both the ideals of the covenant God had made with His people and the failure which king and people made in their moral conduct. The kingdom of sin and Satan was powerful to an extreme. It was the prophets who, with God's help, put some limit to its advances.

Elisha was Elia's assistant, and his master's mantle (symbol of his office) was left to him when Elia disappeared from the face of the earth. Elisha's story, too, is one of opposition to the evil forces of the northern monarchy, but the picture given of him in the Third and Fourth Books of Kings is primarily that of a miracle worker. He restores to life the son of the Shanamite woman (4 Kings 4,25ff.); multiplies loaves of bread to feed a multitude of men (4 Kings 4,42ff.); and cures the leper Naaman of his loathsome disease (4 Kings, chapter 5). In these instances we see the power of God's prophets over death and sickness, two characteristics of Satan's kingdom. In all of this, Elisha is a forerunner of the great prophet, Christ, Who would act in similar fashion.

Amos and Osee (*Read Amos, chapters 1–9;
Osee, chapters 1–14, especially chapters
1–3, chapter 11, and chapter 14*)

These two men are the first of the *writing* prophets, the first of those, that is, whose oracles and sermons have come down to us in written form in books bearing their names. Both prophets had a great deal in common since their ministries were to the northern kingdom of Israel at about the year 750 B.C. At that time Israel was flourishing under the worldly-wise rule of Jeroboam II.

However, in temperament and in emphasis, the two men differed significantly.

Amos was a southerner and a peasant and both facts influenced the presentation of his message. As a southerner, he was not sympathetic to the problems he found in the north; he simply stated and denounced them. As a peasant, he was shocked by the luxury which he found in the thriving cities of Bethel and Samaria. Such richness of material possessions was something new to him, something alien. He mistrusted it from the start. Even more was he shocked to see the cruel discrepancy between the "haves" and the "have-nots," between the grand life of the rich and the abject poverty of the poor upon whom the rich fattened themselves. We have already seen some of his statements regarding social injustice, and can recall his harsh language. Amos speaks to the point; his message is always painfully clear. One can easily imagine the angry reaction of the elegant and gluttonous women of Samaria to Amos' scathing denunciation. Cows, he called them.

> Hear this word, women of the mountain of Samaria,
>   you cows of Basan,
> You who oppress the weak
>   and abuse the needy;
> Who say to your lords,
>   'Bring drink for us!'
> The Lord God has sworn by his holiness:
>   Truly the days are coming upon you
> When they shall drag you away with hooks,
>   the last of you with fishhooks;
> You shall go out through the breached walls
>   each by the most direct way,
> And you shall be cast into the mire,
>   says the Lord (Amos 4,1–3).

True, the language was rough, hardly the kind to make friends and captivate audiences, but for Amos it was the only kind which could point out tellingly the desperateness of the situation. Desperate, indeed, because idolatry was also flourishing.

> Upon garments taken in pledge
>> they recline beside any altar;
> And the wine of those who have been fined
>> they drink in the house of their God (Amos 2,8).

Unless this *social injustice* and *idolatry* immediately ceased to pollute the land, God would destroy the country. This would be a day of judgment, the *Day of the Lord.* Not a happy day of reward and victory as the Israelites hoped, but a day on which the stench of Israel's sins would magnetize upon itself the iron of God's justice.

> Woe to those who yearn for the day of the Lord!
> What will this day of the Lord mean for you?
> Darkness and not light!
> As if a man were to flee from a lion,
>> and a bear should meet him;
> Or as if on entering his house
>> he were to rest his hand against the wall
>> and a snake should bite him.
> Will not the day of the Lord be darkness and not light,
>> gloom without any brightness (Amos 5,18–20)?

And yet, even on the day of judgment, a small group of faithful souls, a *remnant,* would be spared extinction.

> The city that marched out with a thousand
>> shall be left with a hundred,

Another that marched out with a hundred
   shall be left with ten,
   of the house of Israel (Amos 5,3).

In these few citations is contained a fair sample of Amos'
message. It was an outcry against injustice and idolatry as well
as a severe warning of the terrifying day of retribution which
lay ahead from which only a handful (the just) would escape
unharmed. But Amos' work was without success. After a short
ministry of perhaps only a few months, he retired to his simple
life in the Judean hills to the south where he wrote the reflec-
tions which form the body of the book which now bears his
name. He had fought for the ideals of God's covenant with
Israel, had fought and lost. Yet his teaching, his cry for justice
and mercy, his warning of the terrible day of the Lord became
common to the prophets who followed him. It influenced later
generations of Israelites, and carries an important message even
to us of far later, but not much different, times.

Osee spoke to the same people that Amos had denounced,
but the tone of his voice was different. After all, Osee was a
northerner speaking to his own people. His voice was softer
than Amos'; although his criticism was just as strong, it was
uttered with obvious feelings of love and sympathy.

The unique thing about Osee is that he first lived out in his
life the message which he later preached. To explain: Osee
married Gomer, a faithless wife, who soon left her husband for
a life of adultery, perhaps even of ritual prostitution. Osee still
loved her. He searched her out and returned her to his home.
Such was the tragedy of Osee's personal life and such was the
depth of his love for his faithless wife.

Osee preached that same type of tragedy, and that same
depth of love but on a supernatural level. His own misfortune
had helped him to realize the tragedy of Israel's rejection of

God, and the incredible love which God had for Israel. As Osee phrased it, Israel was the spouse of God, united to Him with bonds even closer and more intimate than that of marriage. However, she had been faithless, running heatedly after the pagan gods. Deeper and deeper had she sunk in such spiritual adulteries. In spite of this, God had so often sought her out, had redeemed her and had led her back to Him. God's relationship to Israel had been, on the supernatural level, what Osee's relationship to Gomer had been on the human level.

Could Osee's love for Gomer be explained? Hardly. Love is inexplicable, especially the true love which proves itself with heroic sacrifice. Could God's love for Israel be explained? A few words of this prophet tell us everything we can possibly know.

> I will not give vent to my blazing anger,
> I will not destroy Ephraim (Israel) again;
> For I am God and not man,
> > the Holy One present among you (Osee 11,9).

"I am God and not man"—that is the only possible explanation. God is steadfast in His love because, as a much later inspired writer would tell us, "God is love" (1 John 4,16). God loves because He is love. This is Osee's deepest revelation, a revelation which would be exceeded only when the incarnate proof of God's love hung between earth and heaven to bring salvation to mankind.

Osee, therefore, introduced into the Bible the metaphor of *God's marriage to Israel*. It was a teaching which would be adopted often by later prophets, which would be used by Christ Himself to describe His relationship to the New Israel, the Church, and which would reach its ultimate development in the magnificent Pauline text of Ephesians 5,22–33.

Osee left us another deep spiritual truth in the phrase,

For it is love that I desire, not sacrifice,
and knowledge of God rather than holocausts (Osee 6,6).

In these words Osee took to task the religious formalism of his day, the false religiosity which places its hopes in external ceremonies, multiplying the ceremonial actions instead of acts of love and obedience. What God demanded was merciful kindness, fidelity, and a union with Him which would give knowledge of what He was like. Only as a sign of interior devotion could external sacrifice have validity. Our Lord was to employ these words of Osee when speaking to the religious hypocrites of His own day (Cf. Matthew 9,13;12,7).

The Destruction of the Northern Kingdom of Israel (*Read 4 Kings, chapter 17*)

Amos and Osee both preached to the northern kingdom around 750 B.C. They were God's final messengers to a people who had turned their backs on Him. Amos spoke with words of fire and steel. Osee spoke a language of love. The kings, priests and people shut their ears against both prophets and listened to neither. And so, down upon the northern kingdom came the Day of the Lord, the day of "darkness and not light, gloom without any brightness" (Amos 5,20). God's instrument of justice was the mighty empire of Assyria, with its capital at Ninive, the first of the great world empires. Its control of the Mesopotamian world lasted for almost three hundred years, from about 900–600 B.C.

The last king of Israel, Osee by name (*not* the prophet) ascended the throne about the year 730 B.C. Overcome by the Assyrians under Shalmaneser, King Osee was forced to pay heavy tribute to his conquerers. He turned for help to Egypt. Egypt promised this help but never supplied it in the time of attack. And so Assyria turned on Israel. Samaria, her capital, was placed under siege for three long years, by which time Shalmaneser had died and been succeeded by the famous Sargon, founder of the most powerful of the Assyrian dynasties. In the year 722 B.C. he completely crushed the northern kingdom, exiling the Israelites and planting foreigners "from Babylon, Cuthah, Avva, Hamath, and the Sepharvaim" (4 Kings 17,24) into the territory of Israel. These settled down in northern Palestine, married into the families of any surviving Israelites, picked up a smattering of the Mosaic religion, and evolved into the Samaritans, the hated enemies of the Jews at the time of Christ.

The boastful annals of Sargon describe Israel's end:

In the first year of my reign, I conquered Samaria. I deported 27,-000 people. I took their chariots for my army, I laid tribute upon them. The people of the country, prey in my hand, I made to live elsewhere, and I set my majordomos to govern them, and they payed taxes as people under my rule.[1]

All of this agrees with the sad story told us in the Bible. Carvings, too, exist from the time of Sargon which show us the tragic fashion in which his captives were led into exile. They formed long lines, tied together with cords connecting their wrists or necks, or attached to rings piercing their noses or lips. (Cf. Amos 4,2.) Off went the Israelites to Haran in the north, or over into the Mesopotamian countries to the east. They never returned, the presumption being that they were gradually assimilated into the peoples among whom they were exiled.

And this was so, because the people of Israel had sinned against the Lord their God, who had brought them up out of the land of

1. Daniel-Rop, *Israel and the Ancient World*, (London, Eyre and Spottiswoode, 1948), p. 192.

Egypt from under the hand of Pharao king of Egypt, and had feared other gods and walked in the customs of the nations whom the Lord drove out before the people of Israel, and in the customs which the kings of Israel had introduced. And the people of Israel did secretly against the Lord their God things that were not right . . . and set up for themselves pillars and Asherim on every high hill and under every green tree; and there they burned incense on all the high places, as the nations did whom the Lord carried away before them . . . And they forsook all the commandments of the Lord their God and made for themselves molten images of two calves; and they made an Asherah, and worshipped all the host of heaven, and served Baal. And they burned their sons and their daughters as offerings, and used divination and sorcery, and sold themselves to do evil in the sight of the Lord, provoking him to anger. Therefore the Lord was very angry with Israel, and removed them out of his sight, *none was left but the tribe of Juda only* (4 Kings 17).

In the plan of salvation, only Juda was left. In her and in her kings, the descendants of the Davidic line, was lodged the hope of salvation for Israel and for the nations.

Since the division of the kingdom after the death of Solomon some two hundred years earlier, Juda in the south had been much stabler than Israel in the north. The main reason for this was that, while the kingship in the north belonged to any man strong enough to seize it (often by murder), the southern kingship was a one-family affair. It belonged exclusively to the family of David. This one fact gave it permanence, and stability. In the eyes of the southern citizens their king must be a descendant of David, for thus had God determined through the mouth of his prophet Nathan (2 Kings 7). God had also stated that in some way, at some time, this kingdom would become both universal and eternal. The Judeans knew all of this, were fiercely proud of it and presumed upon it. The thought never entered their minds that just as sin had brought Israel to its sad end, so could sin scatter Juda to the four winds. This possibility did not occur to them; they must remain because their kingdom was eternal.

But serious trouble lay ahead. Even a casual observer of the political and social scene in Juda could see that the sins which had destroyed the kingdom of Israel were the sins of Juda as well. Not quite so pronounced as yet, but definitely present and growing. The same formalism existed, based on the inane trust that the multiplication of animal sacrifices would substitute for the love and obedience that God sought. There were the same social injustices—the inhuman use of one's fellow man for personal profit, injustice to the poor, disregard of the dignity which each man has in God's sight.

And there was the same idolatry: Juda also chased after the pagan gods. Almost at the same time that Israel went into exile, King Achaz of Juda "burned his son as an offering according to the abominable practices of the nations which the Lord drove out before the people of Israel" (4 Kings 16,3). If Juda continued with these immoralities the Day of the Lord would soon fall upon her. Fighting to keep her as the pure bride of God were the prophets of the period, Isaia and Michea and, a century later, Jeremia.

Isaia and Michea (*Read Isaia: chapter 5 (Song of the Vineyard), chapter 6 (Isaia's Vocation), chapters 7–12 (Book of Emmanuel), chapters 33–39 (Ezechia and Sennacherib). Also read Michea: chapters 1–7.*)

Isaia and Michea share a common background. They were both southerners of Juda whose ministries began about the time that those of Amos and Osee finished. Some of their messages were directed to and against the northern kingdom before it fell in 722 B.C. Their main interest, however, concerned the conditions in the kingdom of Juda. In this ministry they were quite successful, mainly because the king who came to power in the south just a few years before (or after—scholars disagree) the fall of Israel was Ezechia, one of the three good kings (David and Josia were the other two) of the monarchy. Isaia, in particular, was a close advisor to King Ezechia who profited immensely by his counsels.

The period of Isaia and Michea was one of turbulence, of political upsets and disorder, of threats and attacks by the Assyrian forces which were now the strongest in the world. Juda was spared the catastrophic destruction of Israel in 722, but the hand of the Assyrians also held Juda in its power even if it did not crush her. After Sargon, the conqueror of Israel, was murdered in 705 B.C., he was succeeded by Sennacherib who began an invasion of Juda about 701. In this he was quite successful, though he did not conquer the city of Jerusalem itself. Either on this occasion, or on a similar one about ten years later (the chronology is difficult to determine) his soldiers surrounded Jerusalem and seemed certain to conquer it, but were then dispersed by what appears to have been a plague. This was a divine salvation for the Judeans, one celebrated in the text of Isaia 37,36–38 and in 4 Kings 19,35–36. Isaia and Michea must be read against this turbulent political and military background.

Very little is known about the personality of Michea or the events of his life. Moreseth, his home town, was some twenty miles southwest of Jerusalem. His simple, unpolished language indicates a man from a humble social position. In this he was similar to Amos, and he was, also like Amos, a man deeply interested in the question of social justice. We have no idea of the length of his prophetic career, nor of the time or circumstances of his death. We read, however, in the book of Jeremia

that at least one of Michea's oracles produced salutary reform
in Juda.

> Michea of Morseth prophesied in the days of Ezechia
>> king of Juda, and said to all the people of Juda; 'Thus says
>> the Lord of hosts,
> Sion shall be plowed as a field;
>> Jerusalem shall become a heap of ruins,
>> and the mountain of the house a wooded height.
> Did Ezechia king of Juda and all Juda put him to death?
> Did he not fear the Lord and entreat the favor of the Lord, and
>> did not the Lord repent of the evil which he had pronounced
>> against them (Jeremia 26,18–19)?

Our information about Isaia is more extensive, though not
nearly so complete as we would wish. His polished Hebrew
indicates a man of culture, and his easy access to both King
Achaz and his son, King Ezechia, shows that he was accustomed
to the circles of the mighty. He was married, and the father of
at least two children. Both of these had symbolic names, the
first Shear-jashub, "a remnant shall return," and Maher-shalal-
hash-baz, "the spoil hurries, the prey hastens." His vocation
to the prophetic life occurred, as he tells us in 6,1 "in the year
King Ozia died." This was about 740 B.C., some eighteen years
before the destruction of Israel. We know that he was still
assisting Ezechia at the time of Sennacherib's invasion about
700 B.C., but have no definite information concerning the end
of his life. A very uncertain tradition says that he was finally
sawed in half by King Manasse, the impious son of Ezechia,
but there is no historical proof for that belief.

Due to the length of these two prophetic careers, especially
that of Isaia, it is not surprising to find great extremes of expression in their writings. There are passages both of consolation and condemnation, for they had to contend, not only with

the good king Ezechia, but also with the notoriously bad king
Achaz, father of Ezechia. Achaz had little faith in Yahweh and
eventually seems to have lost even that little belief that he once
possessed. We know that he sacrificed one of his sons to a pagan
god. Toward the end of his life he went so far as to put a pagan
altar in the Jerusalem Temple. Even the reform period of
Ezechia was by no means completely successful. There was
always plenty of sinful abuse for Isaia and Michea to criticize,
and this they did.

PROPHETIC MESSAGE
OF ISAIA AND MICHEA

These two contemporaneous prophets treat so many points
in common that it is possible to consider them at one and the
same time. In this consideration only the first thirty-nine chapters
of Isaia will be accepted as substantially the work of this prophet.
The later sections of Isaia were written during the Babylonian
exile, some one hundred and fifty years later.

Monotheism is one point of emphasis for both prophets. Isaia
expresses this by pointing out the supreme control that God has,
even over pagan and faraway nations.

> He will give a signal to a far-off nation,
>   and whistle to them from the ends of the earth;
>   speedily and promptly will they come (Isaia 5,26).

In negative fashion both speak out strongly against the idolatry
of their times. It was this, the worst of Israelite sins, that was
forcing divine judgment to manifest itself.

> I will abolish the means of divination from your use,
>   and there shall no longer be soothsayers among you.

I will abolish your carved images
  and the sacred pillars from your midst;
And you shall no longer adore
  the works of your hands.
I will tear out the sacred poles from your midst,
  and destroy your cities (Michea, 5,11–13).

A second point of importance is that of *social justice*. Here
the two prophets agree precisely with their predecessor Amos.
The scathing metaphors used by Michea are the ultimate in
strong language.

Hear, you leaders of Jacob,
  rulers of the house of Israel!
Is it not your duty to know what is right,
  You who hate what is good, and love evil?
You who tear their skin from them,
  and their flesh from their bones!
They eat the flesh of my people,
  and flay their skin from them,
  and break their bones.
They chop them in pieces like flesh in a kettle,
  and like meat in a caldron (Michea 3,1–3).

Interior spirituality, as opposed to external formalism, is another common teaching. This, in particular, indicates the gradual
progress of revelation toward the moment when Jesus would
emphasize the fact that salvation comes through worship of God
in spirit and in truth. Unless external sacrifices are signs of the
offerer's love of God, God has no use for them.

What care I for the number of your sacrifices?
  says the Lord.
I have had enough of whole-burnt rams
  and fat of fatlings;

In the blood of calves, lambs and goats
  I find no pleasure.
When you come in to visit me,
  who asks these things of you?
  Trample my courts no more!
Bring no more worthless offerings;
  your incense is loathsome to me . . .
Your new moons and festivals I detest;
  they weigh me down, I tire of the load.
When you spread out your hands,
  I close my eyes to you;
Though you pray the more,
  I will not listen.
Your hands are full of blood!
  Wash yourselves clean!
Put away your misdeeds from before my eyes;
  cease doing evil; learn to do good.
Make justice your aim; redress the wronged,
  hear the orphan's plea, defend the widow (Isaia 1,11–17).

The idea of a small *remnant* remaining faithful to the Lord in the midst of a sinful nation, and of the same remnant surviving the days of judgment lying ahead, is another teaching which Isaia and Michea share with Amos. All visualize this small group as the future recipients of God's promises, as those to whom and through whom salvation will come.

On that day the Lord of hosts
  will be a glorious crown
  and a brilliant diadem
  to the remnant of his people (Isaia 28,5).

Another even more important truth found in these writings is that of *universalism*, of *catholicism*, in the sense of salvation being in some way extended to the Gentiles. With this we are placed in contact once more with the third of God's promises to Abraham, which spoke of the Gentiles being included in the blessing which had been given to Abraham and his family. Over the course of the centuries this promise, so foreign to the limited outlook of the Israelites, had been largely ignored. It is the prophets who bring it to light and, in so doing, prepare for the coming of Christ's catholic, because universal, kingdom.

In days to come
　　the mount of the Lord's house
Shall be established higher than the mountains;
　　it shall rise high above the hills,
　　And peoples shall stream to it:
Many nations shall come, and say,
'Come let us climb the mount of the Lord,
　　to the house of the God of Jacob,
　　That he may instruct us in his ways,
　　that we may walk in his paths.
For from Sion shall go forth instruction,
　　and the word of the Lord from Jerusalem (Michea 4,1–2; found
　　　　　　　　　　　　　　　　　　　　also in Isaia 2,2–3).

A final enlightening element of these prophets' message was an insistence on *royal messianism,* on the glorious role of the Davidic king who was to come. Isaia lays special emphasis on "the virgin (who) will be with child, and bear a son, and shall name him Emmanuel" (Isaia 7,14). In the chapters following he gives further descriptions of what this king who will bring the presence of God (*Emmanuel* means *God with us*) will be like. He describes him as "a shoot . . . from the stump of Jesse" (11,1), a descendant, therefore, of David whose father was Jesse. Salvation is centered here on an individual, on a royal son of David. In another passage Isaia refers directly to this son of David and to the eternal and universal kingdom promised to him by the prophet Nathan. The description is phrased in such exalted terms that it prepared readers of future generations for a king, the like of whom the earth had never seen.

> For a child is born to us, a son is given us;
>   upon his shoulder dominion rests.
> They name him Wonder-Counselor, God-Hero,
>   Father-Forever, Prince of Peace.
> His dominion is vast
>   and forever peaceful,
> From David's throne, and over his kingdom,
>   which he confirms and sustains
> By judgment and justice,
>   both now and forever (Isaia 9,5-6).

Michea, too, speaks of the awaited Davidic king, of his universal kingdom, and of his mother.

> But you, Bethlehem-Ephratha
>   too small to be among the clans of Juda,
> From you shall come forth for me
>   one who is to be the ruler in Israel;
>   whose origin is from of old,
>   from ancient times.
>   (Therefore the Lord will give them up, until the time
>   when she who is to give birth has borne,
> And the rest of his brethren shall return
>   to the children of Israel.)
> He shall stand firm and shepherd his flock
>   by the strength of the Lord,
>   in the majestic name of the Lord, his God;
>   and they shall remain, for now his greatness
>   shall reach to the ends of the earth;
>   he shall be peace (Michea 5,1–4).

In this quotation it is interesting to note that the future ruler of Israel is described as a shepherd. King-shepherd, an unusual description, but one which would prove itself most accurate in the day of its fulfillment.

The two prophets are intent upon two purposes: to point out current sins to the people of their own days, and to direct their thoughts to the glorious days which lay ahead, somewhere in the future. They caution: Serve God now, respect your neighbor, and thereby you will prepare for the days of the king who is to come. This king will bring salvation, and will usher in a period of peace when men will be God's friends, and friends of each other.

Reign of Manasse, son of good King Ezechia: Interval from Isaia to Jeremia

Manasseh was twelve years old when he began to reign, and he reigned fifty-five years in Jerusalem. His mother's name was Hephzibah. And he did what was evil in the sight of the Lord, according to the abominable practices of the nations whom the Lord drove out before the people of Israel. For he rebuilt the high places which Hezekiah his father had destroyed; and he erected altars for Baal, and made an Asherah, as Ahab king of Israel had done, and worshiped all the host of heaven, and served them. And he built altars in the house of the Lord . . . And he built altars for all the host of heaven in the two courts of the house of the Lord. And he burned his son as an offering, and practiced soothsaying and augury, and dealt with mediums and with wizards. He did much evil in the sight of the Lord, provoking him to anger. And the graven image of Asherah that he had made, he set in the house of which the Lord said to David and to Solomon his son, 'In this house, and in Jerusalem, which I have chosen out of all the tribes of Israel, I will put my name forever; and I will not cause the feet of Israel to wander any more out of the land which I gave to

their fathers, if only they will be careful to do according to all that I
have commanded them, and according to all the law that my servant
Moses commanded them.' But they did not listen, and Manasseh se-
duced them to do more evil than the nations had done whom the Lord
destroyed before the people of Israel. And the Lord said by his servants the prophets, 'Because Manasseh king of Judah has committed
these abominations, and has done things more wicked than all that
the Amorites did, who were before him, and has made Judah also to
sin with his idols; therefore thus says the Lord, the God of Israel. Behold I am bringing upon Jerusalem and Judah such evil that the ears
of every one who hears of it will tingle . . . And I will wipe Jerusalem
as one wipes a dish, wiping it and turning it upside down. And I will
cast off the remnant of my heritage, and give them into the hand of
their enemies, and they shall become a prey and a spoil to all their
enemies, because they have done what is evil in my sight and have
provoked me to anger, since the day their fathers came out of Egypt,
even to this day. Moreover Manasseh shed very much innocent blood,
till he had filled Jerusalem from one end to another, besides the sin
which he made Judah to sin so that they did what was evil in the sight
of the Lord (4 Kings 21,1–16).

This brief description demonstrates clearly how short-lived was
the effect of the good work accomplished by King Ezechia and
the prophets Isaia and Michea. Manasse, son of Ezechia, nullified
that work completely. The extent to which he corrupted the
religious worship of Juda is almost incredible. Pagan altars and
pagan worship in the Temple quarters! If Israel had been
destroyed for her sins, could Juda expect any less severe punishment?

At some point late in the reign of this proverbially evil king
of Juda, probably around 650 B.C., there was born a child named
Jeremia in the small town of Anathoth, a few miles northeast
of Jerusalem. His father, Helcia, was a member of a priestly
family. As a boy, Jeremia lived through the period of religious

decay and perversion sponsored by Manasse. King and people paid no attention to the lesson taught by the destruction of the northern kingdom. They continued to act as though Yahweh did not exist, or, if He did, that He had no personal concern with the moral conduct of His people. God's hand was poised in judgment over the Juda of Jeremia's childhood.

Jeremia (*Read Jeremia 1,4–19* (*Jeremia's Vocation*), *7,1–8,3 and 26,1–19* (*Temple Sermon*), *6,9–12; 15,10–21; 20,7–18* (*Confessions*), *18,1–12* (*Symbol of the Potter's Vessel*), *23,1–8* (*Remnant*), *27,1–22* (*The Yoke Symbol*), *Chapters 30–31* (*Book of Consolation*), *Chapter 36* (*Jeremia's Written Sermons and Joakim*), *and Chapters 37–44* (*Jeremia's Last Years*).)

The perverse Manasse died about ten to fifteen years after Jeremia's birth. Amon, his son and immediate successor, reigned for only a year or two. He was followed by his son Josia, one of the finest of Juda's kings. He was just a child of eight years when he was crowned King of Juda in 638 B.C. During the first years of this boy-king, the impious traditions of Manasse and Amon lived on. The worst type of idolatry flourished throughout the kingdom and in the Temple itself. It must have been obvious to any faithful soul that the country stood in desperate need of a fearless and courageous prophet to proclaim the necessity of conversion. The man was soon to appear on the scene. In the thirteenth year of Josia, 625 B.C., the word of the Lord came to Jeremia summoning him to a prophetic career unique in the experiences of these noble messengers of God. Jeremia's immediate response was reluctant. "Ah, Lord God," he said, "I

know not how to speak; I am too young" (1,6). Jeremia was
not the confident, self-assured type like Isaia. He was a sensitive young man, accustomed to the quiet of small town life,
temperamentally unsuited for the public life and harsh treatment which are the common lot of reformers. Nevertheless
Jeremia did enter into this awesome ministry, buoyed up by
the divine promise of constant assistance.

> See, I place my words in your mouth!
> This day I set you
>   over nations and over kingdoms,
> To root up and to tear down,
>   to destroy and to demolish,
>   to build and to plant . . .
> For it is I this day
>   who have made you a fortified city,
> A pillar of iron, a wall of brass,
>   against the whole land:
> Against Juda's kings and princes,
>   against its priests and people.
> They will fight against you, but not prevail over you,
>   for I am with you to deliver you, says the Lord
>   (Jeremia 1, 9–10 and 18–19).

Some three years later in 622 B.C., Jeremia's task was rendered
temporarily much easier by an extensive reform carried out by
King Josia. This reform was occasioned by the finding of a book
of the Mosaic Law in the Temple. It seems quite certain that it
was some part of the present book of Deuteronomy which was
discovered. When it was read aloud to the young king he was
appalled to realize just how far he and his kingdom had drifted
away from obedience to God's will. A reform was immediately
initiated which must have been a delight to Jeremia's soul.
The description of the reforming measures adopted against

idolatry is absolutely shocking in the picture it gives of Juda's moral degradation.

And the king commanded Hilkiah, the high priest, and the priests of the second order, and the keepers of the threshold, to bring out of the temple of the Lord all the vessels made for Baal, for Asherah, and for all the host of heaven . . . And he deposed the idolatrous priest whom the kings of Judah had ordained to burn incense in the high places at the cities of Judah and round about Jerusalem; those also who burned incense to Baal, to the sun, and the moon, and the constellations, and all the host of the heavens. And he brought out the Asherah from the house of the Lord . . . And he broke down the houses of the cult prostitutes which were in the house of the Lord, where the women wove hangings for the Asherah . . . And he defiled Topheth, which is in the valley of the sons of Hinnom, that no one might burn his son or his daughter as an offering to Molech. And he removed the horses that the kings of Judah had dedicated to the sun, at the entrance to the house of the Lord . . . and he burned the chariots of the sun with fire. And the altars on the roof of the upper chamber of Ahaz, which the kings of Judah had made; and the altars which Manasseh had made in the two courts of the house of the Lord, he pulled down and broke in pieces . . . And the king defiled the high places that were east of Jerusalem, to the south of the mount of corruption, which Solomon the king of Israel had built for Ashtoreth the abomination of the Sidonians, and for Chemosh the abomination of Moab, and for Milcom the abomination of the Ammonites. And he broke in pieces the pillars, and cut down the Asherim . . . (4 Kings 23, 4–14).

No wonder that the prophets spoke out with such force; no wonder that the punishment of God was so severe. Idolatry, perverse fertility rites, and in the Temple itself! How strongly intrenched was Satan's kingdom of sin!

Josia and his reform lasted for approximately thirteen years. In 609 B.C., the king was killed in a battle which appears rather foolish to modern readers. The powerful Assyrian empire had just fallen before the onslaught of the Babylonians; Ninive, the famous Assyrian capital, was destroyed in 612 B.C. However, the remnant of the Assyrian forces reassembled for a final stand. The Egyptian army hastened northward to give aid to the Assyrians, and Josia, foolishly as it seems, attempted to prevent the Egyptian passage through Palestine. He died in the attempt and with his death, the peaceful days of Jeremia's ministry were over. Josia's successors were not kings close to the heart of God, and Jeremia's constant dealings with them were discouraging and ineffectual at best, dangerous to his very life at the worst.

There were four of these successors, but two of them, Joachaz and Joakin, ruled for just a matter of months. Jeremia was to spend most of his time and energy with Joachim and Sedecia. Joakim ruled from 609–598; Sedecia from 598 till the destruction of Jerusalem in 587 B.C. Of these four men Joachaz, Joakim, and Sedecia were the sons of Josia. Joakin was the son of Joakim.

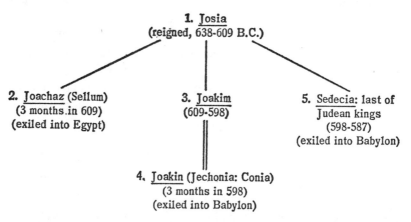

Jeremia's tragic life earned for him the title, "Man of Sorrows." His prophetic career was turbulent, particularly the last twenty to twenty-five years of it. In calling himself a "lamb led to slaughter" (Jeremia 11,19), he unknowingly but truly set himself as a prefiguration of Christ Whose life was also led in the shadow of Jerusalem's approaching destruction. Jeremia's life was one station of the cross after another. His indignation over the moral depravity of Josia's successors and of the priests and people was received with burning resentment. His politically fatuous policy of defeatism in the face of the advancing Babylonians brought the uncontrolled wrath of the kings and military men down on his head. Jeremia's position was not one that could be appreciated except by a man who looked at the world with the eyes of God. As Jeremia saw it, the sins of Juda had tipped the balance beyond recovery. Punishment *must* come from the hand of God, and God had chosen the Babylonians to administer it. The Babylonian army under Nabuchadonosor was simply the justice of God descending upon the sins of Juda. Nothing could stop this punishment, nothing. To resist it, as the kings and generals intended, was to resist God, the worst type of folly. That was Jeremia's view because it was God's. But in preaching it with all his strength, Jeremia's faith was strained to the breaking point.

The prophet is scourged and placed in the stocks (20,2); imprisoned in the quarters of the guards (33,1); beaten and placed in a dungeon (37,15–16). Finally "they took Jeremia and threw him into the cistern of Prince Melchia, which was in the quarters of the guard, letting him down with ropes. There was no water in the cistern, only mud, and Jeremia sank into the mud" (38,5–6). This furnishes the most pathetic image of the suffering prophet, cast out of the world's sight, sinking deeply into the unresisting muck.

There were other painful experiences, too, more of a family nature and, for that very reason, more distressing to the soul of this sensitive man. Jeremia's own kin and fellow-villagers plotted against his safety.

For even your own brothers, the members of your father's house, betray you; they have recruited a force against you (12, 6).

Therefore, thus says the Lord concerning the men of Anathoth who seek your life, saying, 'Do not prophesy in the name of the Lord; else you shall die by your hand' (11,21).

Neither in his father's house, nor in his native village, nor in Jerusalem was there any peace for the despised Jeremia. "A prophet will always be held in honour, except in his home town, and in his own family" is the way that Jesus would describe similar treatment (Matthew 13,57). No wonder that the intimate portrait of his mental anguish given in the chapters called Jeremia's Confessions reveal a man as close to the breaking point as a human can approach. Where was God's help, that very help which God had promised when He called Jeremia to be His prophet? Why was there no respite from the persecution which came from all directions? Why no friendly audiences, no hint of success?

Jeremia almost lost faith, almost gave up. This insight into the frightening trial of a faithful soul is described in passages such as 15,10–18 and 20,7–18 which form part of Jeremia's Confessions.

> You duped me, O Lord, and I let myself be duped;
>   you were too strong for me, and you triumphed.
> All the day I am an object of laughter;
>   everyone mocks me.
> Whenever I speak, I must cry out,
>   violence and outrage is my message;
> The word of the Lord has brought me
>   derision and reproach all the day.
> I say to myself, I will not mention him,
>   I will speak in his name no more.

But then it becomes like fire burning in my heart,
   imprisoned in my bones;
I grow weary holding it in,
   I cannot endure it

Cursed be the day
   on which I was born!
May the day my mother gave me birth
   never be blessed!
Cursed be the man who brought the news
   to my father, saying,
'A child, a son, has been born to you!'
   filling him with great joy.
Let that man be like the cities
   which the Lord relentlessly overthrew;
Let him hear war cries in the morning,
   battle alarms at noonday,
   because he did not dispatch me in the womb!
Then my mother would have been my grave,
   her womb confining me forever.
Why did I come forth from the womb,
   to see sorrow and pain,
   to end my days in shame?
                 (Jeremia 20,7–9, 14–18).

The amazing thing is that Jeremia did not give up. He hoped against hope; he believed when there was no sign of God's presence or God's assistance. He did what he had to do simply because God wanted him to. And all this, remember, without that comforting vision of heavenly joy and peace which we possess, but which was a heavily veiled secret for the Judeans of Jeremia's time. Jeremia continued to suffer for God when the only reward he knew of was one limited to this world, and even that was completely absent from his life. When the "saints come marching in" on the last day, this man of sorrows will certainly be reckoned with the finest.

It might well be that Jeremia's deepest suffering came from the appalling sight of his warnings come true, from the sight of proud Jerusalem destroyed and desolate. In the year 587 B.C., after a fierce siege of about a year and a half, Nabuchadonosor's forces entered Jerusalem and demolished both city and Temple. The sad predictions of Jeremia and his fellow prophets had come true. The "Day of the Lord" had arrived again, the day of just judgment. Juda's sins had forced punishment from heaven; nothing else could have halted her perversions and set her on the rough road to repentance. Jeremia's heart was broken when he saw the city of David and the Temple of the Lord reduced to rubble. When offered his choice of living in honor in Babylon where the Judeans were being exiled or of staying on in the ruins of Juda, he chose the latter. But even there the old man was not to enjoy any peace or rest. His friend, Godolia, whom the Babylonians had appointed governor of the Judeans not taken into exile, was murdered. Fearful of Babylonian reprisals, Jeremia's companions fled into Egypt, against Jeremia's advice, forcing the prophet to accompany them. And there, back in the land from which Moses had delivered the people some six hundred and fifty years earlier, Jeremia had the added sorrow of seeing his fellow Judeans take up with avidity the worship of the idols of the land. When the prophet reproved them, he was given the following answer:

We will not listen to what you say in the name of the Lord. Rather we will continue doing what we had proposed; we will burn incense to the queen of heaven and pour out libations to her, as we and our fathers, our kings and princes have done in the streets of Juda and the streets of Jerusalem. Then we had enough food to eat and we were well off; we suffered no misfortune. But since we stopped burning incense to the queen of heaven and pouring out libations to her, we are in need of everything and are being destroyed by the sword and by hunger (44,16–18).

Such was the final state of Jeremia's life. He died a complete failure in the eyes of the world. He had worked so hard, had suffered so much, and had accomplished so little. It was only in the years that followed his death, as the Judeans exiled in Babylon considered their fate and the teachings of Jeremia, that this remarkable man began to be appreciated. His writings were preserved, his message studied and his teachings applied.

What, in briefest form, was the content of Jeremia's teaching?

Rampant idolatry was the worst eyesore on Juda's horizon. When Joakim had ascended the throne in 609 B.C., the good effects of his father Josia's reforming work were abandoned. Pagan gods were worshipped throughout Juda, even in the Temple. Infant sacrifice was resumed in the valley of Hinnom, just south of Jerusalem. The same religious perversions which had brought divine judgment upon Israel were practiced in Juda. The chastising hand of God could not be far off.

Do you not see what they are doing in the cities of Juda, in the streets of Jerusalem? The children gather wood, their fathers light the fire, and the women knead dough to make cakes for the queen of heaven, while libations are poured out to strange gods . . . The people of Juda have done what is evil in my eyes, says the Lord. They have defiled the house which bears my name by setting up in it their abominable idols. In the Valley of Ben-Hinnom they have built the high places of Thopheth to immolate in fire their sons and their daughters . . . (7,17–18.30–31).

Religious formalism, too, spread like an insidious cancer through Juda's system. We have already seen Jeremia's strong denunciation of Juda's exaggerated trust in the presence of the

Temple in Jerusalem. Her confidence in the physical fact of being God's people, the descendants of Abraham, was also out of order, a useless presumption. What God demanded, said Jeremia, was a spiritual circumcision, a consecration of heart and ear so as to understand God's will and obey it.

> For the sake of the Lord, be circumcised,
>> remove the foreskins of your hearts,
> O men of Juda and citizens of Jerusalem;
>> Lest my anger break out like fire,
> and burn till none can quench it,
>> because of your evil deeds (4,4).

> To whom shall I speak?
>> whom shall I warn and be heard?
> See! their ears are uncircumcised,
>> they cannot give heed;
> See, the word of the Lord has become for them
>> an object of scorn, which they will not have (6,10).

Centuries later St. Paul would insist upon the same truth. "We are the circumcised," he wrote, "we whose worship is spiritual" (Philippians 3,3).

The most important of Jeremia's messages, however, was surely that which concerned the *New Covenant* which God would establish. Jeremia's book is not entirely a warning, a calling to order or a severe denunciation of sin. It also contains some of the most consoling passages in the prophetic books. Chapters 30–31 form the spiritual zenith to Jeremia's oracles, and direct Juda's gaze onto a future of intimate union with God. Jeremia speaks of the new covenant to come, the new religion of the heart and of interior sincerity. This prediction is, indeed, momentous in the evolving history of salvation. The Mosaic covenant bound

Israel to her God in truly magnificent fashion. The Davidic covenant announced by Nathan emphasized the central role of the Davidic king; he would be the special son of God and would someday possess an eternal and universal kingdom. But Israel refused to remain faithful to the covenant with her God and set up altar after altar to the false gods of the pagans. The covenant, therefore, would be abolished. Jeremia's promise of a New Covenant is another in the sequence of arrows pointing to the new religion, the new covenant sealed by the blood of Christ (1 Corinthians 11,25), the new Moses and the Son of David.

The days are coming, says the Lord, when I will make a new covenant with the house of Israel and the house of Juda. It will not be like the covenant which I made with their fathers the day I took them by the hand to lead them forth from the land of Egypt; for they broke my covenant, and I had to show myself their master, says the Lord. But this is the covenant which I will make with the house of Israel after those days, says the Lord. I will place my law within them, and write it upon their hearts; I will be their God, and they shall be my people (31,31–33).

The most obvious thing about Jeremia's preaching was that it was a last warning to the people of his day. His would be God's final word to the people of Juda. If it were not respected and obeyed, disaster must follow.

> Give ear, listen humbly
>   for the Lord speaks.
> Give glory to the Lord, your God,
>   before it grows dark;
> Before your feet stumble
>   on darkening mountains;
> Before the light you look for turns to darkness,
>   changes into black clouds.

> If you do not listen to this in your pride,
>   I will weep in secret many tears;
> My eyes will run with tears
>   for the Lord's flock, led away to exile (13,15–17).

Jeremia offered Juda her last chance, as Amos and Osee had done to Israel. The opportunity was rejected: God's offer was spurned, and His prophet despised. Therefore, in the year 587 B.C., the Babylonians destroyed both city and Temple, and exiled the people into Babylon.

The historical chain of events which lies behind that last sentence is interesting, but we can do scarcely more than sketch it in our rapid treatment of salvation. The Assyrian empire, which controlled the Near East for about three hundred years, began to weaken in the last half of the seventh century B.C. It collapsed before the attack of the Babylonians and Medes in the year 612 B.C. Ninive, its venerable capital, was destroyed and the shattered remains of the Assyrian army gathered at Haran for a futile last stand. It was at this time in 609 that good king Josia was killed trying to prevent the Egyptian forces from proceeding north to aid the Assyrians.

A few years later, 605 B.C., the famous Nabuchodonosor ascended the throne in Babylon, now the seat of world power. Juda was forced to pay tribute to him. When she balked at this, an army was sent to show her the error of her ways. The Judean king of the moment, Joakin, who had just recently replaced his father Joakim, was taken off into Babylon together with a number of the Jerusalem elite. This was the year 598.

The exiled Joakin was succeeded by Sedecia, the last of the kings of Juda. This man was a vacillating character. When Egypt, Tyre and Ammon put pressure on him to league with them in opposition to Babylon, he ignored Jeremia's advice and joined with them. Babylon descended in fury. A siege was laid to

Jerusalem in 588, lasting for eighteen savage months, at the end of which time the Judeans who were shut up inside the city walls were crazed and weak with famine and disease. In 587 the walls were breached. King Sedecia fled toward the desert to the east, but was captured near Jericho and brought to Nabuchodonosor who was residing in his headquarters at Ribla. His sons were killed before him, and then his own eyes were gouged out. The last thing he ever saw was the flowing blood of his children. With that he was led off to Babylon in chains.

In the tenth month of the ninth year of Sedecia, king of Juda, Nabuchodonosor, king of Babylon, and all his army marched against Jerusalem and besieged it. On the ninth day of the fourth month, in the eleventh year of Sedecia, a breach was made in the city's defenses. All the princes of the king of Babylon came and occupied the middle gate . . . When Sedecia, king of Juda, saw them, he and all his warriors fled by night, leaving the city on the Royal Garden Road through the gate between the two walls. He went in the direction of the Araba, but the Chaldean army pursued them, and overtook and captured Sedecia in the desert near Jericho. He was brought to Ribla, in the land of Hamath, where Nabuchodonosor, king of Babylon, pronounced sentence upon him. As Sedecia looked on, his sons were slain at Ribla by order of the king of Babylon, who slew also all the nobles of Juda. He then blinded Sedecia and bound him in chains to bring him to Babylon (Jeremia 39,1–7).

Nabu-zardan, captain of the king's bodyguard, was then sent up to destroy the city of Jerusalem. Israel, both nation and religion, seemed to have come to an end. Kingdom dissolved, city destroyed, Temple flattened to the ground; how devastating the effects of sin!

On the tenth day of the fifth month . . . Nabu-zardan, captain of the bodyguard, came to Jerusalem as the representative of the king of

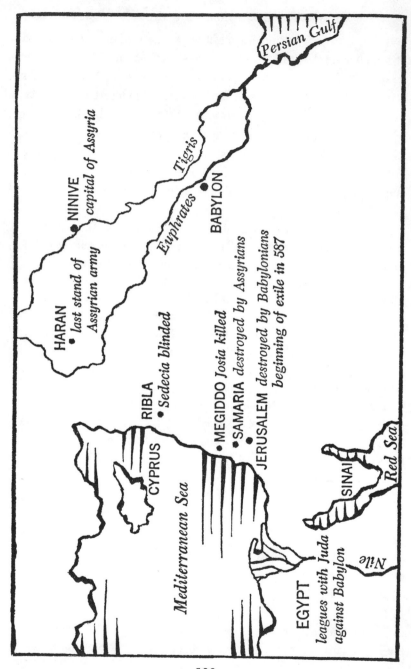

Persian Gulf

NINIVE
capital of Assyria

Tigris

Euphrates

BABYLON

HARAN
last stand of
Assyrian army

RIBLA
Sedecia blinded

MEGIDDO Josia killed

SAMARIA destroyed by Assyrians

JERUSALEM destroyed by Babylonians
beginning of exile in 587

CYPRUS

Mediterranean Sea

SINAI

Red Sea

EGYPT
leagues with Juda
against Babylon

Nile

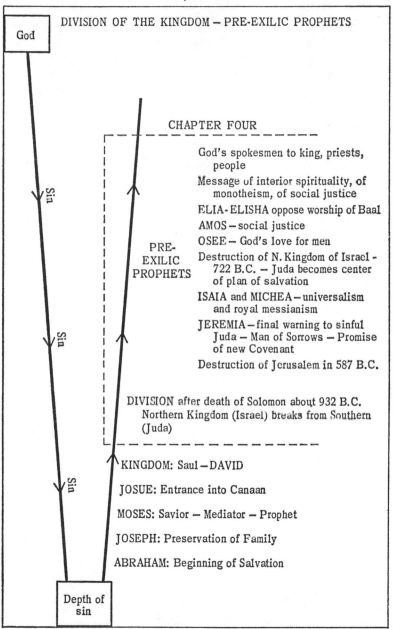

DIVISION OF THE KINGDOM – PRE-EXILIC PROPHETS

God

Sin

Sin

Sin

CHAPTER FOUR

PRE-
EXILIC
PROPHETS

God's spokesmen to king, priests, people

Message of interior spirituality, of monotheism, of social justice

ELIA- ELISHA oppose worship of Baal

AMOS – social justice

OSEE – God's love for men

Destruction of N. Kingdom of Israel - 722 B.C. – Juda becomes center of plan of salvation

ISAIA and MICHEA – universalism and royal messianism

JEREMIA – final warning to sinful Juda – Man of Sorrows – Promise of new Covenant

Destruction of Jerusalem in 587 B.C.

DIVISION after death of Solomon about 932 B.C. Northern Kingdom (Israel) breaks from Southern (Juda)

KINGDOM: Saul – DAVID

JOSUE: Entrance into Canaan

MOSES: Savior – Mediator – Prophet

JOSEPH: Preservation of Family

ABRAHAM: Beginning of Salvation

Depth of sin

Babylon. He burned the house of the Lord, the palace of the king, and all the houses of Jerusalem; every large building he destroyed with fire. And the Chaldean troops who were with the captain of the guard tore down all the walls that surrounded Jerusalem.

Then Nabu-zardan, captain of the guard, led into exile the rest of the people left in the city, and those who had deserted to the king of Babylon, and the rest of the artisans. But some of the country's poor, Nabu-zardan, captain of the guard, left behind as vinedressers and farmers.

The bronze pillars that belonged to the house of the Lord, and the wheeled carts and the bronze sea in the house of the Lord, the Chaldeans broke into pieces; they carried away all the bronze to Babylon. They took also the pots, the shovels, the snuffers, the bowls, the pans, and all the bronze vessels used for service. The basins also, the fire holders, the bowls, the pots, the lampstands, the pans, the sacrificial bowls which were of gold or silver, these too the captain of the guard carried off, as well as the two pillars, the one sea, and the twelve oxen of bronze under the sea, and the wheeled carts which King Solomon had made for the house of the Lord. The bronze of all these furnishings could not be weighed . . . Thus was Juda exiled from her land (Jeremia 52, 12–28).

5

THE EXILE-THE RETURN-
JUDAISM-MACHABEES

SPIRITUAL REVIVAL IN BABYLON

WITH THE DESTRUCTION of Jerusalem and the removal of so many
of its inhabitants into Babylon, our attention turns from the land
of Juda to the land of the exile. We do not know precisely where
the exiles were taken. The earlier ones exiled with King Joakin
in 598 were established mainly near the city of Nippur. Perhaps
some of these who were led captive in 587 ended in the same
locality. The hope of salvation was centered in Babylon, for
Jeremia had quite definitely said that the chosen remnant which
God would rebuild into His people would be those of the exile
rather than the Judeans left back in Palestine.

Thus says the Lord, the God of Israel: Like these good figs, even
so will I regard with favor Juda's exiles whom I sent away from this
place into the land of the Chaldeans. I will look after them for their
good, and bring them back to this land, to build them up, not to tear
them down; to plant them, not to pluck them out. I will give them a
heart with which to understand that I am the Lord. They shall be my
people and I will be their God, for they shall return to me with their
whole heart. And like the figs that are bad, so bad they cannot be
eaten—yes, and thus says the Lord—even so will I treat Sedecia, king

of Juda, and his princes, the remnant of Jerusalem remaining in this
land and those who have settled in the land of Egypt (Jeremia 24,
4–8).

It has been variously estimated that some twenty-five to fifty
thousand Judeans were taken off into the exile. The first stage
of it, the trek of some seven hundred miles into Babylon, must
have been a murderous ordeal, especially for those, such as the
nobles, who were unused to heavy physical work. Only with
difficulty can we begin to imagine the profound discouragement
of this whole sad group. The agony of the long march, and the
debasing life of the concentration camps, were the least of their
worries. The main cross must have been a serious trial of their
faith in God. Where had Yahweh been during the destruction
of Jerusalem, and where was He now? Was there any answer
they could give to the boast of the Babylonians that their god
Marduk must be more powerful than Yahweh? And how could
one account for the luxury of the cities of Babylon and the fruit-
fulness of its country except by postulating the existence and the
protecting hand of a local god like Marduk? It must have seemed
to *many* of the exiles (and the thought must have been a temptation to *all* of them) that the history of their covenant with Yahweh
was a mirage.

The glorious deeds of salvation during the Exodus seemed useless. Maybe they had never happened. Of what value had been
the Temple, the Ark, the priesthood? The Temple was flattened
to the ground, the Ark vanished, the priesthood paralyzed without
the sacrifices for which it had been established. And the Davidic
Kingship to which inspiring promises had been made—what good
had it accomplished? The kings had proved unworthy, perverters
of the Mosaic religion rather than models of its observance.
Joachaz had been taken into captivity in Egypt. Joakin and
Sedecia were slaves in Babylon, the latter a miserable blind man

who could no longer distinguish day from night. There must have been many a weak captive in Babylon who almost lost his faith, and many a weaker who actually did.

This sorrow of the exiles is portrayed vividly in Psalm 136.

> By the streams of Babylon
>   we sat and wept
>   when we remembered Sion.
> On the aspens of that land
>   we hung up our harps,
> though there our captors asked of us
>   the lyrics of our songs,
> and our despoilers urged us to be joyous;
>   'Sing for us the songs of Sion!'
> How could we sing a song of the Lord
>   in a foreign land?
> If I forget you, Jerusalem,
>   may my right hand be forgotten!
> May my tongue cleave to my palate
>   if I remember you not,
>   if I place not Jerusalem ahead of my joy.

Yet from all of this death and misery and discouragement and sorrow God would draw good. The exile was a necessary purification of God's people. Juda had sunk to a low depth of immorality, to idolatry and injustice. What was even worse, the dry-rot formalism that made the practice of religion an hypocrisy and an insult to God had taken root. That had to be cut out; no surface cure was possible. God was the surgeon who had to hurt to cure, and the exile was His scalpel. In Babylon God began the work of renewing, reforming and revivifying His people.

For one thing, the separation from Temple and sacrifice eliminated the formalism connected with these two aspects of religion, and emphasized that which is essential—the total dedication of man to his God. Sacrifices as substitutes for self could no longer be offered: if man was to offer anything in the exile it must be himself.

For another, Yahweh could now be visualized clearly as the God of morality, the God to Whom the actions of men meant something. It is a deep truth, and one which the Israelites often succeeded in ignoring or forgetting, that man's actions have to be measured against the will of God Who determines both good and evil. During the years before the fall of Jerusalem, so very many of Juda's citizens had deluded themselves into believing that Yahweh did not, could not, and should not concern Himself with their private lives. In the reflective years in Babylon they began to see the complete falseness of such a notion. How evident it was to these beaten-down exiles that what man did *was* the concern of man's God, and that what God's people did was His very special concern. A realization of the horror which sin had in God's eyes began to grow, a realization, also, of the awesome power of sin and of the extent to which it had spread over the Israelite world.

The increase in true interior spirituality was accompanied by a new pursuit of study. Deprived of the Temple and sacrifice, the people began to place more emphasis on the understanding and application of God's Word. The ancient writings were gathered together, edited and expanded with care. Writings of the prophets were collected and appreciated for perhaps the first time. A new elite of scribe-lawyers arose who were students of the Law of Moses, the Torah. Their task was to copy and edit and, especially, to study and interpret the old texts. Their leaders were the priests. Energies and time once dedicated to the ritual of Solomon's Temple were now devoted to the formation and study of the Word of God as contained in the traditional books. The Temple was gone; sacrifices were impossible; instruction, study and prayer were their substitutes.

On the human side, credit for Juda's spiritual purification must be given to the earlier prophets, to Jeremia in particular. The words of his warnings still rang in the ears of the exiles and they must surely have realized just how correct those warnings had been. He had even written the exiles a letter of reassurance and of comfort (Jeremia, chapter 29). One paragraph must have been read and reread.

Thus says the Lord: Only after seventy years have elapsed for Babylon will I visit you and fulfill for you my promise to bring you back to this place. For I know well the plans I have in mind for you, says the Lord, plans for your welfare, not for woe! Plans to give you a future full of hope. When you call me, when you go to pray for me, I will listen to you. When you look for me, you will find me. Yes, when you seek me with all your heart, you will find me with you, says the Lord, and I will change your lot; I will gather you together from all the nations and all the places to which I have banished you, says the Lord, and bring you back to the place from which I have exiled you (Jeremia 29,10–14).

The greatest credit for Juda's conversion was due to the prophets of the time, the men who shared the sorrows of the exiles and delivered to them God's message of encouragement, consolation, and instruction. The two most outstanding of these prophets were Ezechiel and Second Isaia.

Ezechiel (*Read chapters 1,1–3,15 (Ezechiel's Vocation), 3,17–21; 14,12–23; 18,1–32; 33, 1–21 (Personal Responsibility), 34,1–16 (the Shepherds), 36,16–37,14 (Resurrection of Juda).*)

This extraordinary man, of even more extraordinary visions, was among the first of the exiles. He was taken away into Babylon in 598 B.C. when King Joakin was exiled. His prophecies date from both before the exile (from 593, the fifth year of Joakin's captivity) and after. In that fifth year, as the prophet himself informs us, "the Word of the Lord came to the priest Ezechiel, the son of Buzi, in the land of the Chaldeans by the river Chobar. There the hand of the Lord came upon me" (Ezechiel 1,3).

Ezechiel's mission was to keep the people's spirits from becoming completely demoralized. Up until the fall of Jerusalem in 587 he prepared his fellow exiles for the shock which that tragedy was sure to bring. He dismissed every false hope, every change of political wind that created wild rumors about the liberation and salvation of the Holy City. It is not so, said Ezechiel. Jerusalem must fall and shall fall: its sins have brought down the punishing hand of God. After the fall, however, as the discouragement of the people rose in proportion to the daily arrival of more hundreds of captives, Ezechiel's function was to bolster the exiles' morale. His message can be reduced to three main points.

First, he insisted on *the omnipresence of God*. Yahweh was not bound to Juda, and Jerusalem, and the Temple. He was not some local deity whose powerful and protecting arm was too short to reach out to the Babylonian towns and hamlets. Juda's God was everywhere. It is this truth which is underlined in Ezechiel's initial vision. As the prophet saw it, the Lord's chariot was mounted on wheels "constructed as though one wheel were within another. They could move in any of the four directions they faced, without veering as they moved . . . Wherever the spirit wished to go, there the wheels went" (Ezechiel 1,16–17. 20).

A second vital truth was man's *personal responsibility* for sin and virtue. Jeremia had already spoken of this (Jeremia 31,29), but Ezechiel insisted upon it to an even greater extent. Whereas past generations had stressed the social unity of the people and the resulting corporate responsibility for sin, Ezechiel emphasizes the other, and equally true, side of the picture. Each man will be responsible for himself. If he is virtuous, he will be rewarded; if he is a man of vice, he will be punished. If he turns from his sins, he will be accepted by God. If he turns from goodness to a life of crime, the reward for earlier goodness will be lost and punishment will await him.

The importance of this simple teaching for the exiles cannot be exaggerated. For if they were to be held responsible for the sins of their predecessors, what hope would there be? What could they do but suffer despairingly? But if, on the other hand, each was to be responsible only for his own deeds, the future could then be different from both past and present. A virtuous life would make each man acceptable to God, and if enough individuals became acceptable to God surely the whole people would begin a new and better era.

Therefore I will judge you, house of Israel, each one according to his ways, says the Lord God. Turn and be converted from all your crimes, that they may be no cause of guilt for you. Cast away from you all the crimes you have committed, and make for yourselves a new heart and a new spirit. Why should you die, O house of Israel? For I have no pleasure in the death of anyone who dies, says the Lord God. Return and live (Ezechiel 18,30–32).

A third, and truly inspiring point, was Ezechiel's *promise of a new Exodus* (this time from Babylon), a return to the land of Juda and a revival of the national and religious life of the people of God. In chapter thirty-four God speaks of renewing the covenant with His people, of becoming again in an effective way their God while they become again His obedient people. He speaks also of His servant David who will be prince over them. This is another reference to the promise of Nathan, but now David is presented, not as a warring and victorious king, but as a *shepherd*. The emphasis has been shifted, surely a providential step in God's work of preparing Israel for the coming of a son of David who would be a shepherd rather than a potentate.

> I will appoint one shepherd over them to pasture them, my servant David; he shall pasture them and be their shepherd. I, the Lord, will be their God, and my servant David shall be prince among them. . . . Thus they shall know that I, the Lord, am their God, and they are my people, the house of Israel, says the Lord God (Ezechiel 34, 23–24. 30).

Chapter thirty-six unfolds a grand summary of the blessings which God promised to His exiled people. God will renew the covenant, this time cleansing His followers, forming a new heart and spirit within them. The basic idea sounds strongly Jeremian and would not be at all out of place even in the New Testament writings.

> For I will take you away from among the nations, gather you from all the foreign lands, and bring you back to your own land. I will sprinkle clean water upon you to cleanse you from all your impurities, and from all your idols I will cleanse you. I will give you a new heart and place a new spirit within you taking from your bodies your stony hearts and giving you natural hearts. I will put my spirit within you and make you live by my statutes, careful to observe my decrees. You shall live in the land I gave your fathers; you shall be my people, and I will be your God (Ezechiel 36,24–28).

Ezechiel's most impressive statement of the "new exodus" theme is found in chapter thirty-seven, the famous vision of the dry bones which come to life. The parable-vision is very clear: Juda in exile is like a field of dry bones. But God would bring them to life, joining bone to bone, filling them out with sinew and flesh, and then breathing life into them.

Surely the hearts of Ezechiel's audience must have increased their beat; the dying embers of hope must have been fanned into flame as the prophet uttered these words of God.

Son of man, these bones are the whole house of Israel. They have been saying, 'Our bones are dried up, our hope is lost, and we are cut off.' Therefore, prophesy and say to them: Thus says the Lord God: O my people, I will open your graves and have you rise from them, and bring you back to the land of Israel. Then you shall know that I am the Lord, when I open your graves and have you rise from them, O my people! I will put my spirit in you that you may live, and I will settle you upon your land; thus you shall know that I am the Lord. I have promised, and I will do it, says the Lord (Ezechiel 37, 11–14).

Ezechiel's preaching was a success. His was the voice which the people heard in the dark days when they had almost given up all hope. He might be called the Joseph of the Babylonian captivity, for he it was who, in the providence of God, had been exiled in advance of his fellow countrymen *to preserve the remnant of Juda* in its faith and trust. He would not live to see the exodus from Babylon, just as Joseph did not witness the return from Egypt. Yet the work of each was necessary for the two returns.

Second Isaia (*Read chapters 40,1–20 (Salvation), 42,1–7; 49,1–6; 50,4–9; 52,13–53,12 (Servant Songs), 42,10–43,21 (The New Exodus), 49,8–50,3 (Restoration of Sion).*)

By "Second Isaia" is meant that anonymous prophet who was responsible for either the final chapters (forty to sixty-six) of our present book of Isaia, or, at least, for chapters forty to fifty-five. He wrote during the exile, somewhere about the year 550 B.C., and was, with Ezechiel, one of the two strong pillars upon which tottering Juda leaned during its years of weakness. His writings are called the "Book of Consolation," an apt title, indeed, for they contain magnificent promises for the future of Juda and of the nations. Our prophet walks in the footsteps of Ezechiel, helping to keep the people's hopes high. One short passage which illustrates this well is chapter fifty-four, verses four to eight. It is very interesting inasmuch as it combines the exodus theme with a theme which appears in Osee, that of Juda as the bride of God. Out of love for His abandoned bride, God will bring the exiles back to their home.

> The Lord calls you back,
>   like a wife forsaken and grieved in spirit,
> A wife married in youth and then cast off,
>   says your God.
> For a brief moment I abandoned you,
>   but with great tenderness I will take you back.
> In an outburst of wrath, for a moment
>   I hid my face from you;
> But with enduring love I take pity on you,
>   says the Lord, your redeemer.

The main contributions which Second Isaia made to the story of salvation can be found in the four *Servant Songs* which do so much to connect Judaism with Christianity which was to be its fulfillment and perfection. These songs are found in Isaia 42,1–7; 49,1–6; 50,4–9; and 52,13–53,12. The first two expand the horizon of salvation by presenting Israel as "the light to the nations," the instrument by which salvation will be mediated to the Gentiles. Previous prophets have already presented the first intimations of this truth, but hardly with the clarity of II Isaia. Perhaps living in peace among the pagan Babylonians enabled this inspired genius to realize the fundamental worth of all men. Made to the image and likeness of God, all men must fit in some way into the plan of salvation.

> Thus says God, the Lord,
>> who created the heavens and stretched them out,
>> who spreads out the earth with its crops. . . .
> I formed you, and set you
>> as a covenant of the people,
>> *a light for the nations* (Isaia 42,5–6).
> You are my servant, he said to me,
>> Israel, through whom I show my glory. . . .
> It is too little, he says, for you to be my servant,
>> to raise up the tribes of Jacob,
>> and to restore the survivors of Israel;
> I will make you *a light to the nations*
>> *that my salvation may reach to the ends of the earth*
>>>>> (Isaia 49,3. 6).

The third song, 50,4–9, speaks of the hostility and persecution which is directed against this Servant of Yahweh. His back is beaten, his beard is plucked, his face spat upon. This presentation prepares us for the sober, inspiring teaching of the fourth Song, a vivid exposé of the *deep truth of expiatory suffering* (52, 13–53,12). The Servant who previously symbolized Israel is now personalized into the figure of one man. This man, though innocent in himself, carries the burden of the sins of mankind. For them he lays down his life and he justifies many by this action, meriting pardon for their offenses. His life is then returned to him, a life of exaltation. To the mind of a Christian this text, written more than five hundred years before the coming of Christ, reads like an apostolic explanation of the meaning of Christ's death and resurrection. This is surely what God intended this passage to mean. The Israel which becomes the light to the nations, salvation to the Gentiles, is the New Israel, Christ Himself, Who won salvation for the many by laying down his life for the sins of all.

> See, my servant shall prosper,
> > he shall be raised high and greatly exalted . . .
> Yet it was our infirmities that he bore,
> > our sufferings that he endured,
> While we thought of him as stricken,
> > as one smitten by God and afflicted.
> But he was pierced for our offenses,
> > crushed for our sins;
> Upon him was the chastisement that makes us whole,
> > by his stripes we were healed.
> We had all gone astray like sheep,
> > each following his own way;
> But the Lord laid upon him
> > the guilt of us all.
> Though he was harshly treated, he submitted
> > and opened not his mouth;
> > like a lamb led to the slaughter
> > or a sheep before the shearers,
> > he was silent and opened not his mouth.
> Oppressed and condemned, he was taken away,
> > and who would have thought any more of his destiny?
> When he was cut off from the land of the living,
> > and smitten for the sin of his people,
> A grave was assigned him among the wicked
> > and a burial place with evildoers,
> Though he had done no wrong
> > nor spoken any falsehood . . .

If he gives his life as an offering for sin,
  he shall see his descendants in a long life,
  and the will of the Lord shall be accomplished through him.
Because of his affliction
  he shall see the light in fullness of days;
Through his suffering, my servant shall justify many,
  and their guilt he shall bear.
Therefore I will give him his portion among the great,
  and he shall divide the spoils with the mighty,
Because he surrendered himself to death
  and was counted among the wicked;
And he shall take away the sins of many,
  and win pardon for their offenses (Isaia 52,13; 53,4–12).

Truly, God writes straight with crooked lines. The destruction of Jerusalem and the Temple, the disappearance of the Ark, the exile of the Judeans—these events seemed like unmitigated evils to the exiles who experienced them. However, during the short stay in Babylon, spirituality, as opposed to mere formalism, came back to life, and to a better life than it had ever lived before in the midst of God's people. Ezechiel and Second Isaia made the main contributions as the dry bones of Israel rose to a new life.

THE RETURN; JUDAISM

Ezra (*Read chapter 1 (Cyrus' Decree), chapter 3 (Rebuilding of Altar), chapters 5–6 (The Second Temple), and chapter 7 (Ezra to Jerusalem).*)

Nehemia (*Read chapters 1–6 (Nehemia and the Walls), and chapters 8–9 (The Solemn Ceremony).*)

"Empires rise and sink like billows, vanish and are seen no more." The Assyrian empire, that awesome power from the east which had taken the northern kingdom of Israel into captivity, vanished in this manner. In time, the Babylonian empire which had been so terrifying a foe at the time of Nabuchadonosor met the same fate. This latter king died about 560 B.C., and about twenty years later Babylon fell before the combined power of the Persians and Medes. Cyrus the Great, King of Persians and Medes, founder of the magnificent Persian empire, entered Babylon in 539. Just one year later, he signed the decree permitting the exiles to return home. He was, indeed, a magnanimous king, careful to respect the customs and deities of the countries subordinated to him. Second Isaia treats Cyrus with special reverence, referring to him as God's shepherd (44,28), and as the annointed of the Lord (45,1).

In 537 B.C., the year after the decree of return was signed, the Jews began to move back to Juda. Not all of them, by any means. Many who had established comfortable homes in Babylon and had prospered in business decided to remain where they were rather than risk the difficult life of returnees. But even these helped the others with generous financial donations. The first group of Jews traveled back home under the leadership of the high priest Josue, and of two survivals of the royal family, Sassabasar (perhaps the son of King Joakin) and Zorobabel, the first governors of the restored Juda. Neither of these royal descendants ever became king. Both were officials appointed by the King of Persia and were definitely dependent on him.

It could not have been long before the Jews who had returned began to doubt the wisdom of their action. What a difficult mess they had stepped into! There was the housing problem first of all. Houses had to be built, or rebuilt, or purchased. Many an heroic soul had to be satisfied with tent accommodations. The hereditary rights to various plots of ground had to be fought out with the Jews and foreigners who had taken over the property during the owners' long absences. Most of the Jews moving in from Babylon must have been young people; persons, consequently, who had never seen Juda before. The shattering contrast between the luxurious cities which they had just left in Babylon and the Judean ruins which now met their eyes must have dispelled any romantic clouds upon which their imaginations floated. The hard facts of life were immediately visible. Juda, their desired homeland, was a poor country, a ruined country, and a tiny country, measuring approximately twenty miles long and twenty-five miles wide. Poor, beaten down, years behind the times!

One of the first things done was to erect an altar on the site of the old one in Jerusalem. A new temple was proposed, and the preliminary work was begun. Enthusiasm soon waned. Seventeen years after the exiles had returned, there was still no temple. But in that same year, 520 B.C., two prophets, *Aggai and Zacharia* (Read Aggai, chapters 1–2; Zacharia, chapters 1–8) succeeded in reviving the people's lost enthusiasm.

Then Zorobabel, son of Salathiel, and the high priest Josue, son of Josedec, and all the remnant of the people listened to the voice of the Lord, their God, and to the words of the prophet Aggai, because the Lord, their God, had sent him . . . Then the Lord stirred up the spirit of the governor of Juda, Zorobabel, son of Salathiel, and the spirit of the high priest Josue, son of Josedec, and the spirit of all the remnant of the people, so that they came and set to work on the house of the Lord of hosts (Aggai 2,12–14).

Five years later the Temple was finally finished. It was built after the plan of Solomon's Temple and was probably the same size as his. Sacrifices were resumed as in pre-exilic times; the priests and Levites took up their liturgical ministries and the

Second Temple (also called the Temple of Zorobabel) became the center of Jewish life. The Ark of the Covenant was missing, but God still certainly recognized the Temple as His home on earth, and the sacrifices offered there would be pleasing in His sight so long as they were true signs of the interior dedication that inspired them.

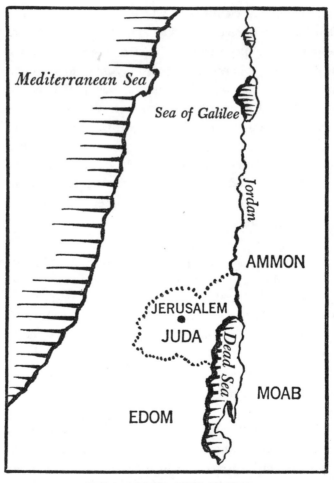

JUDA AFTER THE EXILE

From the year 515 (the date of the completion of Zorobabel's Temple) till the year 445 B.C., there is little information available regarding Juda. It is known that the Samaritans to the north, that amalgamation of Israelites and foreigners which had been planted in the north after the destruction of Israel in 722 B.C., complained with success to Xerxes, then king of Persia, against the rebuilding of the city walls of Jerusalem. As a result, the walls were not rebuilt.

In the year 445, however, there arrived in Jerusalem a layman by the name of *Nehemia.* A Jew himself, he had risen high in Persian political circles and acted as trusted cup-bearer to King Artaxerxes I. He had one definite project in mind, one for which he had received the necessary Persian permission. His project was to rebuild the walls of Jerusalem. He did this in record time. In less than two months after his arrival the walls were up and completed. The speed of this accomplishment seems all the more remarkable when we read that Nehemia's workmen had to serve simultaneously as soldiers, ready to defend the city and its rising walls against surprise attacks by the Samaritans and Ammonites. They worked rapidly, bricks in one hand and sword in the other.

Nehemia's presence in Jerusalem was accompanied, for some time, by that of *Ezra,* the priest-scribe. His contribution to the resurgence of Juda was spiritual. It is clearly described in the eighth and ninth chapters of Nehemia. The eighth chapter tells how Ezra gathered the Judeans about him near the Water-Gate, to the southeast of the Temple grounds. Slowly and distinctly he read to them from the Law of Moses or the Pentateuch, which is the first five books of the Bible. As he read, he paused frequently, giving the Levites time and opportunity to explain to the people the meaning of the passages read. During this whole procedure the people repeatedly cried out their *Amens* to pledge their willingness to abide by God's Law as the law of the nation. The ninth chapter describes another solemn assembly which took place just a few weeks later. On this occasion, Ezra led the people in a solemn ceremony of covenant renewal. He narrated how God had created the world, how He had called Abraham to be the Father of His people, how He had rescued Israel from slavery in Egypt and made it His religious family on Mount Sinai, how He had led it into Palestine and there given it the land promised centuries before to Abraham. Ezra mentioned, too, Israel's constant infidelity to her God, how she had sinned in the desert and how she had sinned in Palestine. At the end of this, Ezra's listeners made a public confession of sins and reaffirmed their willingness to enter anew into their covenant with God.

The scenes described in these two chapters were of deepest meaning for post-exilic Juda, laying the framework for the *Judaism* which lasted till the destruction of both Temple and nation by the Romans in 70 A.D. Père Lagrange has defined this entity in the following fashion:

Judaism was a State constituted by the close alliance of race and religion, of civil and religious legislation in a single law, by the exercise of a single authority, in the hands of the High Priest.

This was the form of the post-exilic Jewish state. In it the King was replaced by the High Priest, who now began to be anointed as had been the pre-exilic kings; the law of the king was replaced by the Law of Moses; the importance of the Ark was replaced by the importance of the sacred Book, the written Word of the Lord. The most sublime vocation, the most elevated activity, was the study of the Law. It was during this time, consequently, that the priests rose to influence and dignity on the one hand, and the scribe-lawyers to an equal rank on the other. *Cult and the Law, the priests and the scribe-lawyers.* If the Temple resumed its position of sacred eminence, the synagogues in which the Law was taught were scarcely less highly respected. Juda had, indeed, a national political governor, appointed by the Persian authorities, but the true leader was the High Priest. Over the years he became more and more the primary figure. His vestments became those previously worn by the Davidic kings, and he himself became the head of the nation and its representative before God.

One last prophetic figure during the early years of *Judaism* was an anonymous personage to whom we have given the name *Malachia.* (Read Malachia, chapters 1–3.) Malachia means simply "my messenger" and has been taken from the opening verse of chapter three, "Lo, I am sending *my messenger* to prepare the way before me" (Malachia 3,1). He can be dated approximately to the time of Nehemia and Ezra, and he gives us an insight into the immorality of the times. Social injustices had risen again to plague the spiritual health of the people. Divorce, which God hates (Malachia 2,16), is another scourge. So too, is the uninspired service of the priests, and the cheap second-rate sacrifices of the people.

Malachia is important in the history of salvation mainly for two items quite special to him. He speaks, first of all, of the *precursor to the Lord,* God's messenger who will proceed the Lord to the Temple. He further identifies this messenger as Elia who will appear before the Day of the Lord.

> Lo, I am sending my messenger
>   to prepare the way before me;
> And suddenly there will come to the temple
>   the Lord whom you seek. . . . (3,1).

> Lo, I will send you
>   Elia, the prophet,
> Before the day of the Lord comes,
>   the great and terrible day,
> To turn the hearts of the fathers to their children,
>   and the hearts of the children to their fathers,

Lest I come and strike
  the land with doom.
Lo, I will send you
  Elia, the prophet
Before the day of the Lord comes,
  the great and terrible day (3,23–24).

A Christian reader will know that it is John the Baptist who fulfills, in a spiritual way, this prediction of the future precursor. In the New Testament his figure is painted against the background of Elia. That prophet's food and clothing are employed by the Baptist who functions as Elia revived in power and spirit.

The second special contribution of Malachia is, perhaps, even better known. It fits into the general context of the third promise made to Abraham: the blessing to be given the nations because of the patriarch's family. Earlier prophets had made this more explicit by extending salvation to the Gentiles. Some such texts have already been cited, e.g., Michea 4,1–2 and Isaia 2,2–3 on page 89. Cf. also the *light to the nations* motif of Second Isaia described on page 129. Malachia makes a further explication. In contrast to the shabby, infirm, blind animal victims being offered at this time, *the Gentiles* will one day offer up to God a continuous sacrifice which will be pleasing to Him. A constant sacrifice, a universal sacrifice, one to be found from the east to the west, from the sun's rising to its setting! And, indeed, when the new covenant was finally struck, the covenant which incorporated the Gentiles into the Body of Christ as spiritual descendants of Abraham, this covenant was established with the blood of a new and spiritual sacrifice which would soon be found represented daily from one end of the earth to the other.

Oh, that one among you would shut the temple gates
  to keep you from kindling fire on my altar in vain!

I have no pleasure in you, says the Lord of hosts;
  neither will I accept any sacrifice from your hands,
For from the rising of the sun, even to its setting,
  my name is great among the nations;
And everywhere they bring sacrifice to my name,
  and a pure offering;
For great is my name among the nations,
  says the Lord of hosts (Malachia 1,10–11).

THE GREEKS AND ROMANS

The Bible is silent about the history of the Jews from the time
of Ezra and Nehemia till the Machabean uprising in 166–165 B.C.
That period of approximately two hundred and fifty years was,
however, one of intense political activity in the world surrounding
Juda. It was the era in which the Persian empire weakened and
crumbled before the vigorous force of the Greeks.

In the year 336 B.C., Alexander the Great, son of Philip of
Macedon, succeeded to the throne of his murdered father. The
young king was only twenty years old, a student of the immortal
Aristotle, and imbued with a philosophy of life hundreds of years
ahead of his time. "All men must become one people," was his
principle. He was the first one-worlder, committed to the attain-
ment of this end even if by the use of force. During his short
reign of some thirteen years (336–324 B.C.) he came remarkably
close to accomplishing his goal.

In 334 he crossed the Hellespont with thirty-five thousand men,
and in the following year he defeated the Persians under Darius.
Intent on attacking the rich Persian province of Egypt, he marched
south into Jerusalem and then down into Egypt. There he was
welcomed by the citizens as a liberator. During the years 332–331
he built the imposing city of Alexandria which soon became one
of the cultural centers of the world. Another victory over Darius

in 331 brought the Persian empire to an inglorious end. Further
east marched Alexander and his soldiers. By 326 he was fighting
an Indian king on the border of India. At this point the army refused to go any further. It had covered some eleven thousand
miles in eight and a half years. In 324 B.C. (some say 323), he died
in Babylon after a short illness; he was still in his early thirties.

Paradoxical as it might appear, Alexander's dream of one world
was eventually brought to a far more successful realization
through the power of prayer and the Spirit than through that of
sword and armor. In the first fifty years after Christ's death, Christianity swept like a wind-driven fire through the world which
Alexander had conquered—Christianity, in which there was
neither Jew nor Gentile, neither slave nor freeman, *but all men
one in Christ.* On the natural level this rapid extension of Christ's
Church owed a sizeable debt to Alexander whose conquests had
spread the Greek language throughout the civilized world of his
time. It was with that language, and because of its universality,
that the first Christian preachers, notably St. Paul, were able to
announce effectively the good news of the world's salvation.

At Alexander's death his empire was divided up among his
generals. To Cassandra was given Macedonia, to Lysimachus
Thraces, to *Ptolemy* Egypt, and to *Seleucus* Babylonia. Only the
latter two are important to our story. General Ptolemy and his
successors (the Ptolemies) created Hellenistic Egypt. For a short
time after the death of Alexander, Palestine was disputed territory, but it was taken over by the Ptolemies in 301 B.C., and
remained under their control till 198 B.C. The sparse sources of
information which are extant indicate that a benevolent rule was
exercised over Palestine. The Ptolemies and the Jews lived on
friendly terms. We know that during this period the Jews formed
a large percentage of the population in Alexandria where they
occupied a position of privilege. It was in that city that the influ-
ential *Septuagint* translation of the Old Testament from Hebrew

into Greek was begun about the year 250 B.C. This work of translation continued for almost two hundred years, and the Septuagint translation rapidly became the Christian Bible in the first days of the Church.

The mild reign of the Ptolemies over Palestine came to an abrupt end in 198 B.C. when Antiochus III, a Seleucid, defeated the Egyptian army. This gave him control of both southern Syria and Palestine. His son was the infamous *Antiochus IV* who ascended the throne in 175 B.C. No false modesty about this man. He entitled himself "Theos Epiphanes"—"God Manifest." The little country of Juda, a tiny island of resistance to the Greek culture which completely surrounded it, infuriated Antiochus. He determined to Hellenize the Jews, to destroy Judaism and the Mosaic Law. Sacrifice was forbidden, as was circumcision. Pork was forced on the populace. In 169, the Temple was robbed, the walls of Jerusalem destroyed and many of the citizens were slaughtered. Two years later the supreme desecration took place. The altar of the Greek god Zeus (Rome: Jupiter; Syria: Baal) was placed over the Jewish altar of holocausts in the Temple, and the Temple itself was made a shrine of the Greek god. This was the desolating sin, the abomination of desolation, spoken of in Daniel 8,13. Never before had the religion of Moses been under such direct and intense attack. All of this makes it easy to understand how the idealistic universalism of the prophets was shelved for an aggressive exclusivism which was considered necessary to keep Juda and its religion alive. Juda turned in on herself, her defense went up, her religious ramparts were strengthened.

The mysterious book of Daniel the prophet must be read against this background of persecution and resistance. It was composed about the year 165 B.C., perhaps right in the midst of the persecution. With regard to the history of salvation it contains one theme of great moment: the *"son of man"* (chapter 7). The most pertinent verses are the following:

As the visions during the night continued, I saw
>One like a *son of man* coming,
>on the clouds of heaven;
When he reached the Ancient One
>and was presented before him,
He received dominion, glory, and kingship;
>nations and peoples of every language serve him.
His dominion is an everlasting dominion
>that shall not be taken away,
>his kingship shall not be destroyed (verses 13–14).

But the *holy ones of the Most High* shall receive the kingship, to possess it forever and ever (v. 18).

Then the kingship and dominion and majesty
>of all the kingdoms under the heavens
>shall be given to *the holy people of the Most High,*
Whose kingdom shall be everlasting:
>all dominions shall serve and obey him (v. 27).

Even a casual reading of these verses must remind us of Nathan's prophecy concerning the everlasting, universal kingdom to be given the Davidic king and, in and through him, to the people of God. In Daniel's vision the king and the people are combined into one figure, as well they might, since the king is the representative of the people, and the people possess the kingdom only in the person of the king. At the same time the title given to the combined king-people is that of "son of man," a definite stress upon the humanity of God's chosen king. In this way, Daniel has managed to mold into one term the messianic characteristics of *Davidic king* and *Servant of Yahweh,* one emphasizing grandeur, the other human lowness. It was this title, "son of man," so rich in meaning, so mysterious at first hearing, that Jesus made His own. In so doing He presented Himself as the Davidic king, representative of the holy ones of the Most High, come to establish an ever-lasting and universal kingdom through the sufferings of His humanity.

In 166–165 B.C., a year after the desecration of the Temple by Antiochus, open revolt flamed out among the Jews. Its leader was Mattathia, a priest from the line of Yehoyarib, an obscure priestly family. The second chapter of First Machabees describes the beginning of the revolt which centered around Mattathias' city of Modin, about 25 miles northwest of Jerusalem. The sons of Mattathias became the military generals. Judas, his third son, but the main military chief from the very start, was called Machabeus, the "hammer," and it is by that name that we designate this family of religious patriots. The dynasty which they established is also called "Hasmonean," perhaps from some ancestor named Hasmon.

The stories of the exploits of the Machabees can be found in the two books of that name, and they match any modern war story in interest and in vivid descriptions. (Read 1 Machabees, chapters 1–16.) It was almost as though the ancient Judges of Israel (the charismatic military chiefs during the days before the kings) had come back to life. The revolt was an immediate success. In December of 165 B.C., Judas took possession of the Temple, instituting the feast of Hannukah, or the feast of Lights, to recall this day of solemn rededication and purification.

The Machabean revolt was not, however, an unqualified *religious* success. It was not long before the successors of Judas proved themselves too worldly, too political, too much like the kings and princes of the Hellenistic world that surrounded Juda. Less than sixty years after the death of Judas Machabeus in 161, his fourth successor, Aristobolus I (104–103) took the title of king. Even worse, the Hasmoneans proclaimed themselves high priests, thus mortally offending many of the legitimately established priests of Jerusalem.

The strongest resistance to those Hasmonean betrayals of the law and spirit of Judaism was registered by the Jews of the most strict observance, those who called themselves the "Hasidim"— "pious ones." This term does not appear to have designated a well-defined sect, but rather the most observant Jews from all strata of society. Many of these Hasidim remained on in Jerusalem, keeping a constant and critical eye on the activities of the Hasmoneans. The Pharisees arose from such an Hasidic milieu. Others, including both priests and laity, renounced entirely the political and religious leadership of the Machabean dynasty and retired into the Judean desert to lead a more spiritual life. Some of them formed the now famous community of Qumran at the northwest corner of the Dead Sea. It was the members of this community who, as the Roman Army advanced in the year 68 A.D. hid their Old Testament manuscripts and their community writings in the nearby cliffs. And there they remained until 1947 when an accidental discovery by an Arab herd-boy brought them out into the world of scholars and journalists. These priceless documents are now known as the Dead Sea Scrolls.

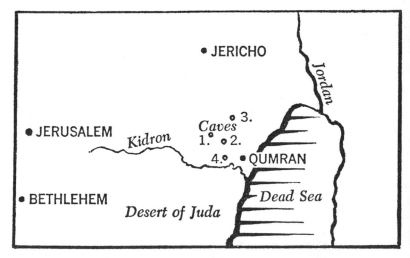

NEIGHBORHOOD OF DEAD SEA SCROLLS

The fifth of Judas' successors, Alexander Jannaeus (103–76 B.C.) was the last important Hasmonean. He was followed by his wife Alexandra who ruled for about nine years. At her death in 67 B.C. the throne and high priesthood were contested by her two sons Hyrcanus and Aristobolus.

Rome steps into the picture at precisely this point. Its international power had been increasing rapidly during the preceding centuries. Carthage had been conquered in 202 B.C., Philip V of Macedonia in 197, Antiochus III in 191. The Near East lay open for conquest.

In 67 B.C., when the two Hasmonean claimants disputed the right to succession, the Romans were called in as peacemakers. Pompey, then at the zenith of his military and political career, encamped with his forces outside of Jerusalem. He was welcomed by Hyrcanus, but Aristobolus and his followers withdrew into the Temple. Battle was begun. It was Aristobolus and the Sadducees against the combined strength of Hyrcanus and the Pharisees and Rome and (an omen of impending doom) the Idumean forces of a man named Antipater. A one-sided contest, to be sure. In 63 B.C., Pompey's forces battered their way into Jerusalem and the Temple quarters. He himself entered into the Holy of Holies. To his surprise, it was empty!

The Roman forces left Jerusalem, but they left it as their vassal. Hyrcanus was installed as high priest, but not as king. Antipater, the half-Jew (the Idumeans had been forcibly judaized and circumcized by an Hasmonean leader some seventy-five years previously) occupied a position of power. Under Julius Caesar (victor over Pompey) Antipater was made procurator of the Jewish State subservient to Rome. His son was Herod the Great, king of the State from 37–4 B.C. He displaced Antigonus Mattathias, last of the Hasmoneans, as high priest, and from that time on the office was at the disposal of the civil authority.

Shortly before Herod's death, Jesus of Nazareth, son of Mary, was born into the world. With him the story of Jewish preparation for salvation comes to its end; with him the story of the accomplishment of Christian salvation marks its beginning.

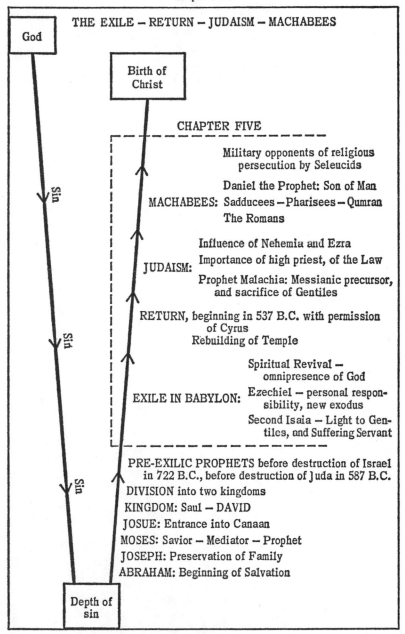

THE EXILE — RETURN — JUDAISM — MACHABEES

God

Birth of
Christ

CHAPTER FIVE

Military opponents of religious
persecution by Seleucids

Daniel the Prophet: Son of Man

MACHABEES: Sadducees — Pharisees — Qumran
The Romans

Influence of Nehemia and Ezra

JUDAISM: Importance of high priest, of the Law

Prophet Malachia: Messianic precursor,
and sacrifice of Gentiles

RETURN, beginning in 537 B.C. with permission
of Cyrus
Rebuilding of Temple

Spiritual Revival —
omnipresence of God

EXILE IN BABYLON: Ezechiel — personal responsibility, new exodus

Second Isaia — Light to Gentiles, and Suffering Servant

PRE-EXILIC PROPHETS before destruction of Israel
in 722 B.C., before destruction of Juda in 587 B.C.
DIVISION into two kingdoms
KINGDOM: Saul — DAVID
JOSUE: Entrance into Canaan
MOSES: Savior — Mediator — Prophet
JOSEPH: Preservation of Family
ABRAHAM: Beginning of Salvation

Sin

Sin

Sin

Depth of
sin

PART 2

NEW TESTAMENT GIFT
OF SALVATION

6

SALVATION ACCOMPLISHED BY CHRIST

THE BASIC OUTLINE of Christ's life is very simple as presented to us by the four Gospels, the Acts of the Apostles, and the various New Testament Epistles. Jesus was born to a virgin named Mary whose husband's name was Joseph. After about thirty years of living an ordinary life as a carpenter's son in Nazareth of Galilee, He began a relatively short career of preaching and healing. His condemnation to death by the Roman official was engineered by citizens of His own nation, the Jerusalem priests and pharisees. Atop a low hill called Calvary, He was crucified with two criminals.

These are the essential facts, minus one, the one that makes all the difference. For Jesus, according to the witness of a courageous group of simple, down-to-earth followers, *rose from the dead.* Of this, these disciples were absolutely certain, certain to the point of devoting the rest of their lives completely to His service, and of laying down those lives in martyrdom as supreme witness to their convictions. Some twenty-five years after the death of Jesus, Paul, a Jew from Tarsus in Cilicia, himself a converted persecutor of the first Christians, wrote down a list of those who had seen Jesus after His resurrection. The list is formidable.

First and foremost, I handed on to you the facts which had been imparted to me: that Christ died for our sins, in accordance with the scriptures; that he was buried; that he was raised to life on the third day, according to the scriptures; and that he appeared to Cephas, and afterwards to the Twelve. Then he appeared to over five hundred of our brothers at once, most of whom are still alive, though some have died. Then he appeared to James, and afterwards to all the apostles. In the end he appeared even to me; though this birth of mine was monstrous, for I had persecuted the church of God . . . (I Corinthians 15,3–9).

Upon the fact of the resurrection was based the faith of the first Christians, and of all Christians after them.

The infant Church, both in its preaching and in its books which contained the first oral teachings in a permanent written form, was not content simply to repeat the external facts of Jesus' life. Led by such excellent theologians as the Apostles John and Paul, she explained the depth of meaning which these facts contained. The meaning which she searched for, found and formulated was derived, not from a consideration of the motives and activities of men, but from revealed knowledge concerning the loving providence of God. What she was looking for was the divine meaning of things.

What did the birth of Jesus mean in the providence of God and in man's relationship to God? What did Christ's miracles mean? His ministry of preaching? His choice of the Twelve? His death on Calvary? His resurrection? What was the relationship of the Church which Jesus had founded to that of the Old Religion founded by Moses in the desert? Questions such as these are answered in the New Testament books. The individual answers furnish the basic ideas which, when arranged in an orderly fashion, produce a biblical theology of the New Testament. The purpose of these chapters is the formalization of such a biblical theology, a systematically arranged account of the meaning of *the life and death and resurrection of Christ* with regard to the work of salvation. To that must be added the role which the Church of Christ, which is His completion as the members are of the body, performs in sharing salvation with individuals, both Jew and Gentile. Finally, we will conclude with a comparison of the two religions which God has given the world, Judaism and Christianity. This comparison must be based on the explanations of Paul for whom this point formed so agonizing a problem.

The entrance of Jesus into the world was an event of inexhaustible depth of meaning. A tiny, very ordinary looking baby born to a young, very ordinary looking mother, and yet heaven and earth, the divine and the human, were joined in this one child who appeared on the stage of human and divine history. *The incarnation of Christ was God's most intimate step into human history.*

God had first demonstrated His supreme control over the world by creating it, thereby manifesting Himself through the works of His hands. He had created mankind upon the earth, mankind made to God's image and likeness. Another divine entrance into history was made in the events which formed the family of Abraham into a people and a religion. These events included the calling of Abraham, the miracle-birth of his son Isaac, the election of Jacob, the preservation of the family in Egypt due to the prestige of Joseph, the summoning of Moses, the plagues, the crossing of the Reed Sea and, in a most particular fashion, the covenant between God and Israel on Mount Sinai. In all of these happenings God entered into world affairs.

In the centuries that followed God continued to act in the interest of His covenanted people. He spoke to them through the written Law begun at the time of Moses, and later expanded and applied to the differing circumstances of Israel's life. He spoke, also, through the mouth of His prophets, encouraging His people, warning them, instructing them. And finally, in a gesture of supremely infinite love and concern, God sent into the hours and seconds of the world's time, into the noise of its cities, into the hills and valleys of its landscape, His only begotten Son. It is this progressive entrance of God into the world that John points out in the first chapter of his Gospel.

When all things began, the Word already was. The Word dwelt with God, and what God was, the Word was. The Word, then, was with God at the beginning, and through him all things came to be; no single thing was created without him. All that came to be was alive with his life, and that life was the light of men. The light shines on in the dark, and the darkness has never quenched it . . . He was in the world; but the world, though it owed its being to him did not recognize him. He entered into his own realm, and his own would not receive him. But to all who did receive him, to those who have yielded him their allegiance, he gave the right to become children of God, not born of any human stock, or by the fleshly desire of a human father, but the offspring of God himself. So the Word became flesh; he came to dwell among us, and we saw his glory, such glory as befits the Father's only Son, full of grace and truth (John 1,1–5. 10–14).

GOD'S LOVE

This incarnate birth of the Son of God was not, needless to say, God's reward to mankind for its sublime acts of virtue. Man's history, as we have seen, was one in which sin seemed his most frequent companion-in-arms. What inspired the incarnation was not man's merit but God's love and mercy. Paul stresses this truth time and again, in terms which show just how awed he was at the thought of God's immense and inexplicable love for sinful man.

But God, rich in mercy, *for the great love he bore us,* brought us to life with Christ even when we were dead in our sins. . . . (Ephesians 2,5).

It is this revelation which has spurred on the martyrs and the other heroic Christian men and women who have dedicated themselves to Christ.

UNITY

What was the purpose of the incarnate coming of God's Son into the world? What was it meant to accomplish? *Unity*, according to the inspired writings: unity of man with his fellow man in Christ, and in Christ with God. Sin had separated man from God —the original sin of Adam and Eve, and the subsequent sins of their descendants. Among men, too, there was a sharp separation, that of Jew from non-Jew. This latter division had been fitted into the overall lines of divine providence by removing the one people of God from the tempting idolatries of the nations that surrounded them. But in itself such a division of man from man was far from being an ideal. It, too, was one of the results of sin, a result typified for us in the story of Cain and Abel. In proportion as man sinned against God and fell away from Him, so would man sin against his fellow man (his brother) and separate from him. Christ's birth was the beginning of the divine ecumenical movement intended to bring men back together with one another, and mutually with God—all this through common unity in Christ. United to Christ we become united to each other, with Christ as the point of union; united to Christ we become united to God, for Christ is God. This is why Christ came into the world, this is the purpose of the Bethlehem manger.

Gentiles and Jews, he has made the two one, and in his own body of flesh and blood has broken down the enmity which stood like a dividing wall between them; for he annulled the law with its rules and regulations, so as to create out of the two a single new humanity in himself, thereby making peace. This was his purpose, *to reconcile the two in a single body to God* through the cross, on which he killed the enmity (Ephesians 2,14–16).

FULFILLMENT

This most personal entrance of God into the world to accomplish man's unity with his brother and with his God did not indicate a completely new plan of divine providence. Christ came, not to destroy the Law and the prophets, but to perfect and complete them. He came to build upon the divine revelation already accorded to the people of the Mosaic religion. He came to fulfill the promises made by God to the heroes of the Old Testament. He came, consequently, as a descendant of both Abraham and of David. To Abraham and his family, his seed, God had promised a blessing, one to be extended through them to the nations. Christ, the descendant of Abraham, would be, in unique fashion, that seed through whom the blessing would go out upon the whole world. To David's descendants had been promised a kingdom both eternal and universal. Christ would inaugurate that kingdom. For these reasons, the Gospel of Matthew presents Christ as son-descendant of both of these grand Old Testament figures.

A table of the descent of Jesus Christ, son of David, son Abraham (Matthew 1,1).

NEWNESS

Christ also brought a radical newness into God's dealings with men. Christianity was not simply the final evolution of Judaism: it was its perfection, its completion, but only by introducing something magnificently novel into the story of salvation. This newness is presented to us in a striking way in the pages of the New

Testament. Matthew, who insists on Jesus' origin from the families
of Abraham and David, is equally insistent on the fact of Jesus'
virginal birth, a birth in which man's role in conception was entirely replaced by the creative power of the Holy Spirit. In Christ
the families of Abraham and David are continued. Yet there is at
the same time a new beginning, a divine re-creation of man.

Mary his mother was betrothed to Joseph; before their marriage she
found that she was with child by the Holy Spirit . . . 'Joseph, son of
David,' said the angel, 'do not be afraid to take Mary home with
you as your wife. It is by the Holy Spirit that she has conceived
this child' (Luke 1,18–20).

MOTHER OF THE LORD

The mother of Christ was a young maiden named Mary. Her
conception and deliverance of the Son of God gives her a most
honored role in the story of salvation, for in a completely unique
fashion salvation entered into the world through her. She, and she
alone, is the mother of the Lord, and it is this, her proudest title,
which we find emphasized in the account of the visitation.

Then Elizabeth was filled with the Holy Spirit and cried aloud,
'God's blessing is on you above all women, and his blessing is on
the fruit of your womb. Who am I, that the mother of my Lord
should visit me' (Luke 1,41–43)?

ARK OF THE NEW COVENANT

Mary's motherhood of her Son Who was at the same time the
eternal Son of God was interpreted with great ingenuity by St.
Luke. In the first two chapters of his Gospel he has emphasized

the similarity between the Virgin Mary and the Old Testament Ark of the Covenant. By this approach, he teaches another aspect of truth inherent in the fact of Christ's incarnation—that in its accomplishment *Mary has become the living Ark of the New Covenant,* the virgin mother whose womb-tabernacle enclosed the glorious presence of God on earth. Luke's Gospel describes the events of the annunciation, and of the visitation to Elizabeth, in phrases and terminology borrowed from those which described the Old Testament Ark. In so doing it tells us in subtle but definite terms of the comparison being proposed.

One striking parallel expression binds together Luke 1,35 and Exodus 40,34–35. In the latter text Moses has just set up the Tent-Tabernacle and placed within it the Ark of the Lord.

Then the cloud covered the Meeting Tent, and the glory of the Lord filled the Dwelling. Moses could not enter the Meeting Tent, because the cloud settled down (*episkiazen,* in Greek) upon it and the glory of the Lord filled the Dwelling.

In Luke 1,35 we read of Mary's divine maternity in words which echo those of the Exodus incident. Mary, too, would be filled with the divine presence through the power of the Most High which would settle down (*episkiasei*—the same Greek verb as in Exodus 40,35) upon her. At this moment of conception she would become the living Ark of God.

Luke is not content to point out the parallel between Mary's annunciation and what was said of the Ark in Exodus. He extends the parallel by underscoring similarities between the Ark's journey to Jerusalem at the time of King David and Mary's journey to Jerusalem for the Presentation. Follow the train of events in the case of David bringing the Ark to Jerusalem from Kiriath-jearim (2 Kings or Samuel, chapter 6) and that of Mary carrying her God from Nazareth to Jerusalem, and note the similarities which Luke points out to him who thinks in Old Testament terms as he reads. As David and his people rejoice in the presence of the Ark (2 Kings, or Samuel, 6,12–15), so do Elizabeth and her child in the presence of Mary (Luke 1,44). As David leaps in joy before the Ark (2 Kings, or Samuel 6,16), so does the still unborn John the Baptist before our Lady (Luke 1,44). The outcry of the people of Israel (2 Kings, or Samuel 6,15) is echoed by that of Elizabeth (Luke 1,42). As the Ark remained in the house of Obededom for three months (2 Kings, or Samuel 6,10), so did Mary in the house of Zachary (Luke 1,40). And Elizabeth's expression in Luke 1,43, "Who am I that the mother of my Lord should visit me?" reads like a conscious paraphrase of David's query, "How can the Ark of the Lord come to me" (2 Kings, or Samuel 6,9)?

Certainly Luke's purpose throughout all this is clear, even if this echo-technique is unfamiliar to modern readers. His purpose is to teach us that Mary is the Ark of the New Covenant, which he accomplishes by describing this short period in Mary's life against the background of the Old Testament story of the Ark of the Covenant. Parallels are emphasized by using similar or identical phraseology. The author paints the scene as much by looking at the past as by gazing on his present facts. This literary procedure is called *midrashic*, a meditation on contemporary events in the light of already composed scriptural texts.

THE POOR—THE GENTILES

Two final scenes connected with the birth of Christ have an importance which goes far beyond the obvious content of the stories. These are the descriptions of the first pilgrimages made to the crib of the incarnate Son of God. One visit was made by the shepherds of the fields (Luke 2,8–20), the other by the Magi from the east (Matthew 2,1–12). In these incidents the gospel writers have seen typified the solemn entrance of the poor (the shepherds) and the Gentiles (the Magi) into the friendship of God which this child brings about. The infant has been sent by God to bring good news to the poor and afflicted (Isaia 61,1), and to be the light of salvation to the Gentiles (Isaia 42,6; 49,6).

The next significant phase in the life of Jesus was His apostolate. Introduced by the preparatory preaching of John the Baptist (the precursor foretold by Malachia 3 and Isaia 40,3–4), Jesus exercised His public ministry as *teacher* and *miracle worker.* The evangelists, Matthew in particular, have thrown light on the meaning of both of these roles.

TEACHER

As teacher, says St. Matthew, Christ is the New Moses. The first Gospel gives special emphasis to this identification because it is particularly interested in offering Christianity to the Jews in a way which will make it as appealing and persuasive to them as possible. To first-century Jews reluctant to make the leap from Judaism to Christianity, the Church presented the New Moses, Christ. He had come, not to destroy Moses and his work, not to undermine the rightful prestige of the Old Testament mediator, but to bring the religion of Moses to its promised perfection by elevating its commands and teachings to an unexpected grandeur. Just as Moses was the outstanding prophet of the Old Covenant and the most exceptional of the messengers through whom the Lord's word had come to the people, Christ had come as the prophet of God, the messenger through whom God would speak His final word. This presentation of Christ as the prophet greater than Moses must have been commonplace to the apostles since it finds place in the Temple sermon of Peter as recorded in the Acts of the Apostles.

Repent then and turn to God, so that your sins may be wiped out. Then the Lord may grant you a time of recovery, and send you the Messiah he has already appointed, that is, Jesus. He must be received into heaven until the time of universal restoration comes, of which God spoke by his holy prophets. Moses said, 'The Lord God will raise up a prophet for you from among yourselves as he raised me; you shall listen to everything he says to you, and anyone who refuses to listen to that prophet must be extirpated from Israel' (Acts 3,19–23).

Also, just as Moses was the unexcelled lawmaker of the Old Religion, Christ, the New Moses, is depicted by Matthew as the new and supreme lawmaker. It is for this reason that Matthew places such heavy emphasis on the Sermon on the Mount. In his Gospel it occupies the whole of chapters five to seven. Luke treats it in a much briefer fashion in the second half of chapter six. Mark does not mention it at all.

Matthew wants his readers to see clearly the lawmaker parallel. Just as Moses ascended the mount of Sinai to give the Old Law, Christ ascended the lakeside mountain to deliver the New Law, one incomparably superior to that of Moses. This New Law calls blest the poor, the sorrowful, the meek, the just, the merciful, the simple, the peacemakers, the persecuted. It insists on the internal dispositions of men rather than on external practices, on the spirit which should inspire alms, prayers and fastings more than on the actions themselves. Above all, it demands a constant and perfect practice of universal love and in this, particularly, does the New Law of Christ differ sharply from the Mosaic Law which was based solidly on the virtue of justice.

You have learned that they were told, 'An eye for an eye, and a tooth for a tooth.' But what I tell you is this: Do not set yourself against the man who wrongs you. If someone slaps you on the right cheek, turn and offer him your left. If a man wants to sue you for your shirt, let him have your coat as well. If a man in authority makes you go one mile, go with him two. Give when you are asked to give; and do not turn your back on a man who wants to borrow. You have learned that they were told, 'Love your neighbour, hate your enemy.' But what I tell you is this: Love your enemies and pray for your persecutors; only so can you be children of your heavenly Father, who makes his sun rise on good and bad alike, and sends the rain on the honest and the dishonest (Matthew 5,38–45).

With this, Christ, the New Moses, changes the old law of justice, the law of "mine and thine" to the law of love, the law of "neighbor first."

MIRACLE WORKER

Christ's apostolate was distinguished by miracle working as well as by teaching. In these miracles, also, the evangelists have discovered deeper meanings. Mark presents them as "eye-openers," as the means by which the apostles discovered who Jesus of Nazareth was. When they first began to follow Him, it must have been mainly His forceful personality and dynamic preaching that drew them. But as the weeks went by and they saw with their eyes the wonders which He worked, and heard with their ears the sublime truths which He taught, they began to wonder and to discuss who this man might be. We see this clearly in Mark's description of the miracle of the calming of the waves.

A heavy squall came on and the waves broke over the boat until it was all but swamped. Now he was in the stern asleep on a cushion; they roused him and said, 'Master, we are sinking! Do you not care?' He stood up, rebuked the wind, and said to the sea, 'Hush! Be still!' The wind dropped and there was a dead calm. He said to them, 'Why are you such cowards? Have you no faith even now?' They were awestruck and said to one another, 'Who can this be whom even the wind and the sea obey' Mark 4,37–41)?

This is a typically Markan presentation of the meaning and value of the miracles. By them, step by step, the apostles were led to the point where they believed with firm faith that this former carpenter, this magnificent teacher and worker of miracles, was in fact the long awaited Messiah, the Christ.

'And you,' he asked, 'who do you say that I am?' Peter replied: 'You are the Messiah' (Mark 8,29).

St. John has a quite different theology of Christ's miracles. He sees them as *signs*, as wonders which could be observed on the natural level by everyone possessing physical eyesight, but which were symbolic of similar truths on the supernatural level which only the eyes of faith could perceive. Thus, for John, the miracle of the multiplication of the loaves in chapter six of his Gospel was meant to symbolize the most important of all bread miracles, that of the Eucharist, the supernatural bread which would feed the souls of men. The miracle by which the man born blind (chapter nine) received sight upon washing in the pool of Siloam symbolized the supernatural truth that Christ was the light of the world. It was a sign, too, that this Christ-light would be given through a washing in water, baptism. The miracle of the restoration of Lazarus to life (chapter eleven) is presented by John in the same context in which Jesus calls Himself the life of the world. A person united to Christ will, in fact, never die. In this world as in the next his life will be joined to the eternal life of God. Such is the use which John makes of Christ's miracles, such the hidden significance which he finds in them.

The story of salvation is especially illuminated, however, by Matthew's interpretation of the miracles. He portrays them as the direct attacks made by Christ on that kingdom of Satan from which man must be saved. As previously noted, the kingdom of Satan is characterized by four elements: by *Satan* himself, by *sin* which takes rise from him as its source, by *death* which sin brings, and by *sickness* which so often preludes death. Satan, sin, death, and sickness: the four voices which moan the dirge of damnation. In chapters eight and nine Matthew has linked together a whole series of miracles, ten in all. With the exception of one, the calming of the storm on the lake, all of these are attacks on Satan's kingdom and proof positive of Christ's power over it, a power which will effect its supreme victory at the conclusion of Christ's life. Jesus cures the *sickness* of leper, of the centurion's servant, of Peter's mother-in-law, of a paralytic at Capharnaum, of the woman with the hemorrhage, and He restores sight to two blind men. Moreover, he casts *Satan* out of demoniacs, *brings back to life* the daughter of the synagogue official, and *forgives the sins* of the paralytic. Every characteristic of Satan's kingdom is encountered and vanquished. For Matthew this was the evidence that the kingdom of Satan was losing its hold on the world, that the kingdom of heaven was now at hand in the person of Christ. It also meant, so far as salvation was concerned, that as Satan's kingdom weakened and the kingdom of heaven grew in power, the work of salvation was about to be accomplished. Christ expressed all this quite simply:

But if it is by the Spirit of God that I drive out the devils, then be sure that the kingdom of God has already come upon you (Matthew 12,28).

Christ's teaching, then, points to Him as the new Moses. His miracles indicate the arrival of the kingdom of heaven in which will be found the power to overcome that of Satan.

FOUNDER OF A PERMANENT INSTITUTION

One final aspect of Christ's apostolate must be stressed. During His short public life He began to prepare for a permanent institution which would survive His temporary physical life on earth. He had no intention of limiting His teaching and His salvific power to the period during which He walked the roads of Palestine. He purposed to leave behind Him a new organism, the new People of God, the new Israel, in which both his teaching and power would continue. Therefore, we find Him gathering together a small group of especially chosen men. There were twelve of them. We call them the first apostles but their earliest name was "The Twelve."

This number was not simply a matter of chance due to the fact that only those twelve happened to measure up to the high requirements for discipleship. On the contrary, the number *twelve* was required by the fact that the Old Testament People of God had had twelve patriarchs. As Christ began to establish the new Israel He wanted twelve men to replace the patriarchal sons of Jacob-Israel. By this very fact He showed His intention of founding something of permanent nature, a new People, a new Israel. That the apostolic Twelve understood this is clear from the necessity they felt to elect someone to fill the place of Judas after his defection (Acts 1,21-22). This symbolism of the twelve apostolic patriarchs of God's new People also helps us understand the following statement of Christ:

> you shall eat and drink at my table in my kingdom and sit on thrones as judges of the twelve tribes of Israel (Luke 22,30).

The choice of the Twelve was only one step in the inauguration of the new Israel. During His apostolate Christ began to provide also for the spiritual welfare of this new Israel by promising, or alluding to, certain means which would communicate the Spirit and weaken the strength of Satan's kingdom.

He proclaimed the necessity of a spiritual rebirth through a washing in water joined to the power of the Spirit.

In truth I tell you, no one can enter the kingdom of God without being born from water and the spirit (John 3,5).

He also permitted his disciples to administer a preparatory baptism similar to that employed by John the Baptist.

After these things Jesus and his disciples came into the land of Judea, and he stayed there with them and baptized. . . . When therefore, Jesus knew that the Pharisees had heard that Jesus made and baptized more disciples than John—although Jesus himself did not baptize, but his disciples—he left Judea and went again ino Galilee (John 3,22; 4,1-2).

The miracles which we have seen recounted in Matthew, chapters eight and nine, were interpreted by that evangelist as evidence of Jesus' power over the kingdom of Satan and proof that the kingdom of God had come into the world. We are likewise told by the Gospel writers that Jesus did not reserve this power to Himself, but that *He began to share it with His apostles.* He sent them out into the surrounding villages and there, besides proclaiming the arrival of the kingdom of God, they also exercised the spiritual strength which Christ had given them for curing sickness and casting out Satan.

Then he called his twelve disciples to him and gave them authority to cast out unclean spirits and to cure very kind of ailment and disease (Matthew 10,1).

They drove out many devils, and many sick people they anointed with oil and cured (Mark 6,13).

In this way Christ prepared His chosen Twelve for the profound participation in His power which would be theirs after His glorification. That power would be applied in many ways. It would enable them to repeat the saving sacrifice of Christ and forgive sins, the deepest possible sharings in Christ's authority over Satan's kingdom. It would enable them also to heal the various sicknesses which take their first origin from the sin of man. All such power would be, of course, shared—a power which would be that of Christ, but which would flow from Him into His living helpers.

Another act of importance for the permanent character of the new People of God was Christ's abolition of divorce. In the interest of a firmer family union (upon which the People of God must depend), and with the will to restore marriage to its original ideal condition, Christ terminated the divorces permitted by Mosaic Law. Such an abolition would work a deep effect on the character of the New Israel.

The question was put to him: 'Is it lawful for a man to divorce his wife?' This was to test him. He asked in return, 'What did Moses command you?' They answered, 'Moses permitted a man to divorce his wife by note of dismissal.' Jesus said to them, 'It was because you were so unteachable that he made this rule for you; but in the beginning, at the creation, God made them male and female. For this reason a man shall leave his father and mother, and be made one with his wife; and the two shall become one flesh. It follows that they are no longer two individuals: they are one flesh. What God has joined together, man must not separate.' When they were indoors again the disciples questioned him about this matter; he said to them, 'Whoever divorces his wife and marries another commits adultery against her:

so too, if she divorces her husband and marries another, she commits adultery (Mark 10,2–12).

With this restoration of marriage to its ideal form, Christ prepared for the amazing parallel which Paul would draw between the union of man and wife and that between Christ and His Church. (See pages 184–185.) Surely, if marriage were not a "till death do us part" institution, it could hardly be compared to the eternal union between Christ and His People. Paul's striking analogy, for which Christ's abolition of divorce was a necessary preparation, would reveal to the Church the stability and holiness of the union of man and wife in the Lord.

Christ also promised that the Spirit of God would be given to the New Israel. We have already seen His reference to baptism in water and the Spirit in John 3,5 (see page 156), and it is that same Gospel which tells of Christ's assuring pledge to His apostles that they would soon receive the Spirit of Truth to transform them into witnesses to Him. This was a preparation for the visible conferring of the Spirit on Pentecost, for the invisible conferring on Easter Sunday (John 20,22–23), and for the imposition of hands by which the apostles themselves granted the Spirit of witness to the first Christians.

But when your Advocate has come, whom I will send you from the Father—the Spirit of Truth that issues from the Father—he will bear witness to me. And you also are my witnesses, because you have been with me from the first (John 15,26–27).

So Peter and John laid their hands upon them (the newly baptized of Samaria) and they received the Holy Spirit (Acts 8,17).

In one other way did Christ lay the ground-work for the spiritual life of the Church He was bringing into existence. He promised that He would feed it with a bread from heaven which would be His own body and blood. Not only did He promise supernatural food (John 6); He worked a miracle to forecast it: the multiplication of bread. This, as has been pointed out already (see page 153), was selected by John as one of the sign-miracles. Just as Christ possessed the power over bread to multiply it according to man's needs, so also did His power extend over the same bread to change it into His own body and to offer it as food for the spiritual hunger of all men of all times. Although the Gospel of John underlines this teaching in more obvious fashion than do the other Gospels, yet even in these latter we cannot help but notice that the multiplication of bread is described in terms which remind us immediately of the Last Supper. Christ, says St. Mark, took bread in His hands, looked up to heaven, blessed, broke, and gave to His disciples (Mark 6,41). This description must bring thoughts of the Eucharist to the mind of any Christian reader. (See Matthew 15,36.)

In conclusion, then, we can determine the following important aspects of Christ's apostolate. *His teaching* was His acceptance of the role previously held by Moses. He had come as greatest of all *prophets*, the incarnate Word of God bearing God's final word of revelation to the world. In a manner surpassing that of Moses, He had also come as the new *Law-giver*, and this law could be reduced to one command—love. He called for a truly interior dedication to God, for which the phrase, "utter and undying love," seems the only sufficient description.

Jesus came, likewise, as a *miracle-worker*. In the theology of St. Matthew we find these miracles interpreted as direct attacks on the horror kingdom of Satan, sin, death, and sickness. In this perspective, the miracles were proof that the kingdom of Satan was receding before the kingdom of God.

Finally, Jesus' apostolate was devoted to the establishment of the *permanent framework and sources of life of the new Israel.* "The Twelve" were chosen to replace the Old Testament patriarchs. Christ's power over Satan was shared with His apostles.

They began to cure demoniacs and to heal the sick. At that early stage, there is no indication that they shared in the ultimate power over Satan, that of forgiving sins, and surely they did not possess it at that time. It was the next step in the progressive participation that they enjoyed in the power of Christ. We find Jesus speaking of a future baptismal rite, and we read of the apostles administering something similar to it. By abolishing divorce Christ eliminated a root danger to the social health of the New People of God, and perpared for the comparison Paul would make between the union of Christ and Church and that of man and wife. Christ also promised the supreme gift of the Holy Spirit, as well as a bread which would feed His People. This bread, he insisted, would be His own body, and the drink which would accompany it would be His own blood.

At this point in the Gospel description of the work of our Lord, salvation had not yet been effected. But the kingdom of God had arrived in the person of this Son of God and son of Mary, the battle between the kingdom of God and that of Satan had begun, and the foundation had been laid for the permanent establishment of the New Israel, the New People of God, based firmly on "The Twelve" who had already to share the power of Christ.

The actual work of salvation was accomplished at the very end of Christ's life on earth. His conflict with the prince of darkness which was so evident throughout the whole of His apostolate came to a climax on the hill of Calvary. That was "the hour" spoken of so often in the Gospel of St. John, the hour for which the world had been waiting since the fall of our first parents, the hour in which the power of Satan would yield to the power of Christ, the new Adam. It was of this hour that Christ had spoken:

Now is the hour of judgement for this world. Now shall the prince of this world be driven out (John 12,31).

VICTORY OVER SIN

What was it in Christ's death that cancelled out the sin of mankind? The writings of John and Paul answer this question for us. We know, first of all, that the original sin of Adam and Eve, as well as the subsequent sins of their descendants, was a manifestation of the two basic vices present in every sin, *pride* and *disobedience*. It is always man's inordinate love for his personal gratification which leads to the disobeying of God's law. These two sources of moral evil are presented clearly to us in the Genesis description of man's fall. The temptation speaks of man becoming like God; this is the appeal to his pride. The act performed is forbidden by God; here is the disobedience. Each subsequent sin in the story of mankind followed a similar pattern. In Christ's death for the sins of men, however, we observe an absolutely opposite procedure. Christ dies as the supreme manifestation of self-giving love (the opposite of self-loving pride) and of complete obedience to the will of God. Virtue cancels out vice. The love and obedience of the new Adam satisfy for or blot out the pride and disobedience of the old Adam.

The love and obedience involved in Christ's death for sin are expressed frequently and in varying fashions by John and Paul. The love involved in Christ's death was two-fold. It was the *love of God the Father for men,* a love so infinite that it led Him to send His Son into the world to effect man's salvation.

For God is love; and his love was disclosed to us in this, that he sent his only Son into the world to bring us life (1 John 4,9).

At the same time, the crucifixion was the supreme demonstration of *Christ's love for sinful mankind.*

Live in love, as Christ loved you, and gave himself up on your behalf as an offering and sacrifice whose fragrance is pleasing to God (Ephesians 5,2).

Obedience, too, is stressed in the New Testament descriptions of Christ's death. Paul states that the disobedience of Adam which resulted in our becoming sinners has been replaced by the obedience of Christ, the new Adam, which makes us just.

For just as through the disobedience of the one man the many were made sinners, so through the obedience of the one man the many will be made righteous (Romans 5,19).

It is Paul, likewise, who has handed on to us the inspiring Christian hymn which extols the humility of Christ as manifested in an obedience which led him to the depth of disgrace, death by crucifixion.

He humbled himself, and in obedience accepted even death—death on a cross (Philippians 2,8).

John has left us a passage in which both aspects of this victory of virtue over vice are stressed, in which both the love and obedience of Christ are regarded as the opponents of Satan.

The prince of this world approaches. He has no rights over me, but the world must be shown that I love the Father and do exactly as he commands (John 14,30–31).

In all of this we find the inspired explanation of Christ's death as being victory over sin. He conquered the devastating force of sin's basic vices, pride and disobedience, by the most magnificent demonstration of love and obedience which the world has ever seen. In this sense the hour of Calvary was an hour of victory and an hour of glory. John's Gospel, in fact, describes it as the hour of Christ's glorification. The glorification consisted in this supreme manifestation of the virtues of love and obedience—of self-giving love, of life-renouncing obedience. Such was Christ's victory over sin.

VICTORY OVER DEATH

The work of salvation cannot, however, be limited to Jesus' death for sin through the noblest possible exercise of love and obedience. There is another essential aspect to it. The main characteristics of Satan's kingdom were two-fold, sin and death. Christ's sacrifice of self had scored the victory over sin. *It was His resurrection that conquered death.* Rising up from the earth on the third day, He broke death's power over men born of women. Just as the first Adam had brought death upon his descendants, so the second Adam guaranteed future life to all who would accept the life flowing from His glorified body.

For since it was a man who brought death into the world, a man also brought resurrection of the dead (1 Corinthians 15,21).

For he has broken the power of death and brought life and immortality to light through the Gospel (2 Timothy 1,10).

By reflecting on the victorious resurrection of Christ, Paul was able to scoff at death. For him it held no terror. Christ had died and had risen. He, Paul, would die one day, but it would be like the death of Christ, a passage from this world into one of incomparable splendor and happiness. Why, then, fear death? The tragedy of it was erased for all those willing to profit by the resurrection of Christ.

Death is swallowed up; victory is won! O Death, where is your victory? O Death, where is your sting? The sting of death is sin, and sin gains its power from the law; but, God be praised, he gives us the victory through our Lord Jesus Christ (1 Corinthians 15,54–57).

Salvation consists precisely in Christ's sacrificial death for sin and His resurrection victory over death. In satisfying for sin and overcoming death Christ toppled the kingdom of Satan, and it was from that kingdom that we needed to be saved. When we speak of the work of salvation, consequently, we must remember that there were *two* aspects to it: Christ's death and His resurrection. Paul says that

He was delivered to death for our misdeeds and raised to life to justify us (Romans 4,25).

Paul depicts Christ's victory over Satan in terms which remind us of the Roman emperors returning from victorious battles, their conquered victims dragged along in chains behind them. In similar fashion, Satan is bound in chains for all who share the death and resurrection of Christ.

On that cross he discarded the cosmic powers and authorities like a garment; he made a public spectacle of them and led them as captives in his triumphal procession (Colossians 2,15).

The story of Christ's death and resurrection should recall to mind the portrait of II Isaia's Suffering Servant. (See page 119–120.)

> Though he was harshly treated, he submitted
>   and opened not his mouth;
> like a lamb led to the slaughter
>   or a sheep before the shearers,
>   he was silent and opened not his mouth . . .

Through His suffering, my servant shall justify many,
and their guilt he shall bear . . .
Because he surrendered himself to death
and was counted among the wicked;
And he shall take away the sins of many
and win pardon for their offenses (Isaia 53,7. 11–12).

This is indeed a magnificent description of the expiatory value
of Christ's death and His victory over sin, penned some five hundred years before the fact. The same song by Second Isaia refers
also to the reward of the Servant, his return to life. In so doing it
ties together death and resurrection as happened in actual fact
to Jesus.

See, my servant shall prosper,
he shall be raised high and greatly exalted . . .
If he gives his life as an offering for sin,
he shall see his descendants in a long life,
and the will of the Lord shall be accomplished through him.
Because of his affliction
he shall see the light in fullness of days . . . (Isaia 52,13;53,10–11)

The idea of Christ as the Suffering Servant Who laid down His
life for His people and was restored to life Himself was a prized
and common possession of the first Christians. Peter refers to
Christ as the *Servant* in his Temple sermon in Acts 3,13 and 3,26.
Philip the deacon evangelizes the official of the Queen of Ethiopia
by explaining to him how Christ was the fulfillment of the text
we have just seen concerning the lamb led to slaughter, the sheep
quiet before its shearers. Paul gives us the same interpretation in
an early Christian hymn which stresses both the humiliation and
subsequent exaltation of the Servant, the man of sorrows.

Bearing the human likeness, revealed in human shape, he humbled
himself, and in obedience accepted even death—death on a cross.

Therefore God raised him to the heights and bestowed on him the name above all names, that at the name of Jesus every knee should bow—in heaven, on earth, and in the depths—and every tongue confess, 'Jesus Christ is Lord,' to the glory of God the Father (Philippians 2,7–11).

WOMAN OF THE VICTORY

It is with regard to Christ's sacrificial death for sin that reference is made in John's Gospel to the woman who gave Him human life.

When Jesus, therefore, saw his mother and the disciple standing by, whom he loved, he said to his mother, '*Woman* behold thy son.' Then he said to the disciple, 'Behold thy mother.' And from that hour the disciple took her into his home (John 19,26–27).

Down through the centuries readers of this passage have wondered at the term by which our Lady is addressed. "Woman," to be sure, is not a term of disdain. Yet it is a strange way for a son to address his mother, nor can we find any parallel in Jewish literature to indicate that at the time of Christ a son ever spoke to his mother in this fashion. To make the problem more acute, in the story of the changing of the water to wine at Cana we find the same manner of address on Jesus' lips. "Woman" is the title He gives to Mary in both passages. Why?

The solution to this problem is derived from the *clear interest that John's Gospel has in the book of Genesis.* The most obvious example of this can be found in the very first chapter of the Fourth Gospel. There the opening words, "In the beginning," are the same as those with which the book of Genesis starts. This is of special significance to a Jewish reader because, for him, the title of the book was always taken from its opening words, just as is the case today for the papal encyclicals. When he heard

the first words of John's Gospel, "In the beginning," he must
have thought immediately of the other book with the same opening phrase which formed its title, the book of Genesis. After its
Genesis-like beginning, the Gospel goes on to speak of creation, as
does the book of Genesis, and the distinction of light from darkness, just as Genesis does. There are numerous other contacts
between Genesis and John, but these must suffice to show John's
interest in the first book of the Bible, and in its early chapters
especially. It is because of this clear interest that the possibility
emerges that perhaps the "woman" of John's Gospel is in some
way related to the "woman" of Genesis 3,15. In that passage, as
has been already noted (see page 15), God speaks of the future
conflict between Satan and his seed and the "woman" and her
seed. He speaks also of a time in which the woman's seed will
be wounded in the heel while Satan shall be wounded in the
head. As we read through John's Gospel we can see clearly that
John has this very conflict in mind, and that he presents the
battle between Christ and Satan as the fulfillment of the warfare
spoken about in the book of Genesis. John quotes Christ to the
effect that,

Now is the hour of judgement for this world; now shall the Prince of
this world be driven out (12,31).

He also tells of Satan's influence in contriving Christ's crucifixion.

The devil had already put it into the mind of Judas son of Simon
Iscariot to betray him (13,2).

He also describes Satan's seed who aid him in this battle
against Christ. This seed includes those who range themselves
against Jesus: Judas and the Pharisees. Judas is actually called
a devil.

'Yet one of you is a devil.' He meant Judas, son of Simon Iscariot. He it was who would betray him. . . . (6,70–71).

The Pharisees, for their part, are told that the devil is their father because, like them, his nature is false and murderous.

'Your father is the devil and you choose to carry out your father's desires. He was a murderer from the beginning, and is not rooted in the truth; there is no truth in him' (8,44).

This conflict between Jesus, the woman's seed, and Satan and his seed reaches its climax on Calvary where Christ is wounded unto physical death. This death wins the grand victory over sin. At that moment of warfare, John notes for us all the participants in the battle predicted back in Genesis 3,15. The woman's seed, Jesus, is there, as are Satan and his seed. Even the garden locale is duplicated, for

at the place where he had been crucified there was a garden, and in the garden a new tomb, not yet used for burial (19,41).

We must explain Jesus' use of the term "woman" for His mother against this background. Surely it must indicate that Mary is the divinely intended woman of the conflict, the mother of sorrow who is at the same time and by the same token, the woman of the victory. She stands beside her son, her seed, at the moment of His bruising, which is the moment of His victory. With Him she shares the pain and the suffering; with Him, too, she shares the victory. It is Mary's share in the victory of Christ over sin and death which forms the theological basis for the Spirit-inspired Church's belief in her Immaculate Conception (a complete victory, through Christ, over sin) and in her Assumption (her victory, as closest associate with Christ, over death).

MOTHER OF MEN, THE NEW EVE

John tells us something else, too, in the text we have just seen. This is concerned with the presentation of Mary as mother to the disciple whom Jesus loved. John's Gospel is one of *signs,* in the sense that he often mentions human, visible things which are symbols of somewhat similar, but much more important, spiritual realities. Thus, the multiplication of the bread in chapter six was a sign of the Eucharist. The cure of the man born blind in chapter nine was a sign that Jesus is the Light of the world and that His light is given initially in baptismal washing. The cure of Lazarus in chapter eleven was a sign that Jesus is the Life of the world. It appears most probable that the presentation of Mary as mother to the disciple whom Jesus loved is another sign, a sign of our Lady's spiritual motherhood of Jesus' disciples. John is chosen as the exemplar since he is the disciple whom Jesus loved with a special love, the disciple who participated the more intimately in Jesus' life by resting on His breast, by sharing the sorrows of Calvary, by being present at the effusion of the Spirit (19,34). The selection of John at this time highlights the fact that Mary's maternity is in the order of love, that those who love her Son the more are, by that fact, the more her children. The deepest teaching of this Johannine sign is that Mary has become the new Eve, taking the place of the wife whom the first Adam had named "Eve because she was the mother of all the living" (Genesis 3,20).

CHRIST GLORIFIED AND THE SPIRIT

The exposition to this point shows that Christ toppled the kingdom of *Satan* through His sacrificial death for *sin* and His resurrection from *death*. There is one more important point to be stressed with regard to Christ's resurrection. In itself it was, of course, the definitive victory over death. At the same time it was the more positive beginning and source of supernatural life. Christ rose, not to the same human life which He had previously possessed, but to one in which His human nature was the living concentrate of the Holy Spirit. Jesus rose in His glorious body, and that glorious body was the instrument through which the Spirit would be poured forth upon the faithful. The image projected in the New Testament writings presents the risen Christ as glorious in a human nature now spiritualized, from Whom the Spirit flows out upon the world.

John's Gospel states that the Spirit could not be given until Christ had been glorified (John 7,39). The moment of that glorification, and of the beginning of the era of the Holy Spirit was the moment of Jesus' death. As His side was pierced, blood and water flowed out. The water is a Johannine symbol of the Spirit, and at this moment John sees symbolized the effusion of the Spirit upon humanity from the body of Christ. This symbolic interpretation is justified by John's earlier explanation:

On the last and greatest day of the festival Jesus stood and cried aloud, 'If anyone is thirsty let him come to me; whoever believes in me, let him drink.' As the Scripture says, 'Streams of *living water shall flow out from within him.' He was speaking of the Spirit* which believers in him would receive later; for the *Spirit had not yet been given, because Jesus had not yet been glorified* (John 7,37–39).

Once Christ has been glorified by His death and resurrection He begins immediately to communicate the Spirit. This He does first of all to the apostles on the evening of Easter Sunday.

Late that Sunday evening . . . Jesus came and stood among them . . . Jesus repeated, 'Peace be with you.' . . . He then breathed on them, saying, 'Receive the Holy Spirit! If you forgive any man's sins, they stand forgiven; if you pronounce them unforgiven, unforgiven they remain' (John 20,19–23).

On Pentecost Sunday, fifty days later, the Spirit was poured out upon the disciples and manifested openly to the world. This event fortified the first Christians as witnesses to Christ and constituted the external inauguration of the reign of the Spirit which is contemporaneous with the Kingdom of God on earth.

Paul, in particular, emphasizes the role of the Spirit in the world's salvation. United to Christ Who pours forth the Spirit, we become *shrines, temples of the Spirit and sons of God.*

Your body is a shrine of the indwelling Holy Spirit, and the Spirit is God's gift to you (1 Corinthians 6,19).

The Spirit you have received is . . . a Spirit that makes us sons, enabling us to cry 'Abba! Father!' (Romans 8,15).

To be reborn as sons of God a *new source of life* is needed. The Spirit provides this, elevating man to a new and higher level of existence.

If the Spirit is the source of our life, let the Spirit also direct our course (Galatians 5,25).

. . . you are on the spiritual level, only if God's Spirit dwells within you (Romans 8,9).

Dwelling within us, effecting our spiritual rebirth, the Spirit also *guides and directs our conduct.* Thus, Romans 8,4 speaks of

. . . us whose conduct, no longer under the control of our lower nature, is directed by the Spirit.

His guidance is to be sought and accepted in all things, but particularly for our prayers.

. . . the Spirit comes to the aid of our weakness. We do not even know how to pray, but through our inarticulate groans the Spirit himself is pleading for us (Romans 8,26).

Since it is the Spirit that unites us to Christ, it is the Spirit also *who unites us to each other in Christ.* He is our source of unity.

Spare no effort to make fast with bonds of peace the unity which the Spirit gives (Ephesians 4,3–4).

. . . we are all brought into one body by baptism, in the one Spirit, whether we are Jews or Greeks, whether slaves or free men, and that one Holy Spirit was poured out for all of us to drink (1 Corinthians 12,13).

Finally, the gift of the Spirit is *God's assurance,* His pledge, the foretaste of the *even more glorious life* which awaits the faithful in the next world.

. . . it is God also who has set his seal upon us, and as a pledge of what is to come has given the Spirit to dwell in our hearts (2 Corinthians 1,22).

The discussion of the Holy Spirit at this point has, to an extent, entered into the material which will constitute the next division, the sharing by the individual Christian in the salvation accomplished by Christ. However, this treatment has served to emphasize that the risen Christ, glorified through His death and resurrection, was the mediator of the Spirit. His glorification was not for himself but for us.

7

SALVATION SHARED

ALTHOUGH CHRIST WON the victory over Satan's kingdom of sin and death, it nevertheless remains true that not by that glorious fact is everyone personally saved. We can still lose our souls. The question rises, then, and it would be difficult to think of one more urgent and serious: How can we be saved? How can we share in the salvation effected by Christ?

SALVATION IN CHRIST

The fundamental truth with regard to personal salvation is that only in Christ, through union with Him, can a man be saved. Salvation can be found in Christ, and there only. Salvation is the unique individual possession of one man, the God-man, Who is the perfect and only necessary mediator between God and man. He alone has conquered sin and death; He alone has won the victory. All others simply share it, and that sharing is solely through union with Him. This is perfectly clear in the New Testament writings. The following citations, one from Paul, the second from Peter in the Acts, the third from our Lord Himself in the Gospel of John, are simply three different ways of stating the same basic truth.

For there is one God, and also one mediator between God and men, Christ Jesus, himself man, who sacrificed himself to win freedom for all mankind (1 Timothy 2,5).

There is no salvation in anyone else at all, for there is no other name under heaven granted to men, by which we may receive salvation (Acts 4,12).

I am the way; I am the truth and I am life; no one comes to the Father except by me (John 14,6).

UNION WITH CHRIST

If salvation can be found only in Christ, how can we be united to Him so as to share the salvation He has won? What unites us to Christ, the one mediator between God and men? These questions are not easy to answer—they cannot be answered in any one word. The biblical evidence shows that there are a small number of essential elements which combine to effect our union with Christ. No one New Testament writer ever synthesizes all of this for us. That we must try to do for ourselves, working with the individual truths which have been handed down to us in the inspired books. From these it is certain that the following elements are the essential ones for effecting union with the risen and Spirit-giving Lord.

FAITH. For the first Christians this one simple word had a complexity of meaning. First of all, it was a *gift*, pure and simple, not due to human nature or to any individual man. This gift was primarily intellectual; it was *belief* in Jesus as the Christ, as the Son of God, as the risen Lord. During Christ's lifetime He had demanded a similar faith. He inquired of the apostles what they believed Him to be. Their answer, expressed by Peter, was that He was the Christ (Matthew 16,16; Mark 8,29; Luke 9,20).

Through the light of subsequent happenings, especially the resurrection, ascension, and Pentecost, the apostles realized that Jesus was more than the awaited Messiah, that He was in an absolutely unique fashion the Son of God and that He was the Lord of the universe, God Himself. These basic truths were the nucleus of the Christian faith. One simple expression of them is found in St. John's Gospel:

Those here written have been recorded in order that you may hold the faith that Jesus is the Christ, the Son of God, and that through this faith you may possess eternal life by his name (John 20,31).

The briefest of all Christian creeds was simply "Jesus is Lord." This was a direct statement of belief in the divinity of Christ, connected directly or indirectly with faith in Christ's resurrection, which is the supernatural and historical foundation of Christianity.

If on your lips is the confession, 'Jesus is Lord,' and in your heart the faith that God raised him from the dead, then you will find salvation. For the faith that leads to righteousness is in the heart, and the confession that leads to salvation is upon the lips (Romans 10,9–10).

The complex little word, "faith," also meant the *acceptance of Jesus* as savior. Salvation could not be found in the Law or in the works of the Law. It could not be found in any human works. Salvation could be found only in Christ, through Him, because of Him. We cannot save ourselves. Even the good works that we perform are, in reality, the good works which Christ works in us. It was this insistence on Christ alone as savior which gave the first Christians their powerful feeling of *hope*. How great a savior they had in Christ! And how much God loved them by sending them so magnificent a redeemer! If God had loved them so much while they were still in their sins, who could possibly measure the love He had for them now?

But God, rich in mercy, for the great love he bore us, brought us to life with Christ even when we were dead in our sins, it is by his grace you are saved. And in union with Christ Jesus he raised us up and enthroned us with him in the heavenly realms, so that he might display in the ages to come how immense are the resources of his grace, and how great his kindness to us in Christ Jesus. For it is by his grace you are saved, through trusting him; it is not your own doing. It is God's gift, not a reward for work done. There is nothing for anyone to boast of. For we are God's handiwork, created in Christ Jesus to devote ourselves to the good deeds for which God has designed us (Ephesians 2,4–10).

Faith, then, as presented in the New Testament writings, includes belief, acceptance, and hope. In a sense, it must also suggest love, for how could one so hope and believe in Jesus the risen Lord without loving Him?

Consequently, faith is an essential means of union with Christ. In fact it is the primary, for all else builds upon it. For this reason Paul has much to say about it. His letters to the Romans and to the Galatians are concerned primarily with this one point. Also, because of this truth, he places great emphasis on Abraham, the father of believers. He says very simply that faith has always been the means to salvation. Just as Abraham was saved by believing and trusting in the things that God told him, so also all who are saved will find their redemption by following Abraham's example.

SACRAMENTS. The sacraments are a second essential element for entering union with Christ, and of them, Baptism and the Eucharist receive special treatment in the inspired writings

Baptism is described in various fashions by the New Testament authors. In John 3,5 it is called a rebirth, without which a person cannot enter into the kingdom of God.

In truth I tell you, no one can enter the kingdom of God without being born of water and spirit.

The same is true of Titus 3,5. But it is especially in the letters to the Romans and to the Colossians that Paul writes a magnificent theology of baptism. For him it effects a *union with Christ who died and rose.* Through this spiritual union with Christ Who died and rose, the Christian dies and rises. He dies to sin and rises to a new life. This is his sharing in Christ's victory over sin and death. Paul begins with the historic death and resurrection of Christ. These were the two sides of the coin of salvation. That historical death and resurrection effect, for those united to Christ by baptism, a corresponding sacramental death and resurrection. The new Christian, in Christ, is thereby saved from the kingdom of sin and death, is transferred over into the kingdom of God, and begins the life in the Spirit which is concentrated in the risen Lord.

Have you forgotten that when we were baptized into union with Christ Jesus we were baptized into his death? By baptism we were buried with him, and lay dead, in order that, as Christ was raised from the dead in the splendour of the Father, so also we might set our feet upon the path of life. . . . For in dying as he died, he died to sin, once for all, and in living as he lives, he lives to God. In the same way you must regard yourselves as dead to sin and alive to God, in union with Christ Jesus (Romans 6,3–4. 10–11).

For in baptism you were buried with him, in baptism also you were raised to life with him through your faith in the active power of God who raised him from the dead (Colossians 2,12).

The *Eucharist* is the most evident means of union with Christ, for in It we receive His body and blood (Matthew 26,26–28; Mark 14,22–24; Luke 22,19–20; 1 Corinthians 11,23–25; John 6,50–58). This is our supernatural food, our means of life, one which sustains us during our period on earth and insures eternal life hereafter. Christ's insistence on it as a necessary element for union with Him is most emphatic.

In truth, in very truth I tell you, unless you eat the flesh of the Son of Man and drink his blood you can have no life in you. Whoever eats my flesh and drinks my blood possesses eternal life, and I will raise him up on the last day. My flesh is real food; my blood is real drink. Whoever eats my flesh and drinks my blood dwells continually in me and I dwell in him. As the living Father sent me, and I live because of the Father, so he who eats me shall live because of me. This is the bread which came down from heaven; and it is not like the bread which our fathers ate: they are dead, but whoever eats this bread shall live for ever (John, 6,53–58).

In addition to uniting us to Christ, this sacrament unites us with one another by joining us to one common point, the risen body of Christ present in the Eucharist.

The bread that we break, is it not a sharing of the body of Christ? Because the bread is one, we, though many, become one body, for we all share the one bread (1 Corinthians 10,16–17).

CHARITY. Charity is the third of the essential elements which unite us to Christ and to the salvation which He extends. John has stressed this more than any other writer.

God is love; he who dwells in love is dwelling in God and God in him (1 John 4,16).

Anyone who loves me will heed what I say; then my Father will love him, and we will come to him and make our dwelling with him (John 14,23).

John is retracing with firmer step the path of revelation trodden centuries before by the prophet Osee. That messenger of God also spoke mainly of the love which God had for Israel, His faithless spouse. How to explain it? Only with the divine words: "For I am God and not man" (Osee 11,9). God loved because that is what He is—love. Christ, the God-man, is love, too, and the manifestation of God's love for the world. In love, then, we must be united to Christ, and in Him to God.

Faith, the *sacraments* of Baptism and the Eucharist, *Love:* these uniting elements are supremely important in the eyes of the New Testament theologians. Paul, who speaks so often about them, is certain that all of them are absolutely necessary, all are inter-related. Faith, for example, is intimately related to Baptism.

For in *baptism* you were buried with him, in baptism also you were raised to life with him through your *faith* in the active power of God who raised him from the dead (Colossians 2,12).

For through *faith* you are all sons of God in union with Christ Jesus. *Baptized into union with him,* you have all put on Christ as a garment (Galatians 3,26–27).

Faith, in turn, is related to love. Paul says:

. . . the only thing that counts is *faith active in love* (Galatians 5,6).

Paul connects faith with hope and love, and gives superiority to love.

In a word, there are three things that last forever: faith, hope, and love; but the greatest of them all is love (1 Corinthians 13,13).

Finally, Baptism and the Eucharist are joined together in a number of passages. The flow of water and blood from the pierced side of Christ may well be a Johannine symbol of these two sacraments of salvation (John 19,34). And Paul has written a passage in which he speaks of the Israelites' passage through the Sea and their consumption of the miraculous food and drink of the desert as symbols of Christian Baptism and Eucharist. He joins these together.

Our ancestors were all under the pillar of cloud, and all of them passed through the Red Sea; and so they all received baptism into the fellowship of Moses in cloud and sea. They all ate the same supernatural food, and all drank the same supernatural drink (1 Corinthians 10,1–3).

EFFECTS OF UNION

United to Christ by *faith,* the *sacraments,* and *love,* we become *individually:*

joined to God the Father. This is the whole purpose of salvation: that man, who had fallen from the original goodness which was his in union with God, should be brought back into life-giving contact with it once more. In Christ this union is restored.

Christ was innocent of sin, and yet for our sake God made him one with the sinfulness of men, so that in him we might be made one with the goodness of God himself (2 Corinthians 5,21).

temples of the Holy Spirit Whom Christ mediates in our souls.

Do you not know that your body is a shrine of the indwelling Holy Spirit, and the Spirit is God's gift to you (1 Corinthians 6,19).

citizens of heaven because our source of life is divine, our conduct is regulated by the Holy Spirit, and our promised goal is eternal life.

We, by contrast, are citizens of heaven, and from heaven we expect our deliverer to come, the Lord Jesus Christ (Philippians 3,20).

brothers of Christ Who is joined to us by supernatural links forged by the Holy Spirit. United to us, Christ works constantly to shape us after His own pattern. Christ Himself appears in the life of a man completely dedicated to His will.

For God knew his own before ever they were, and also ordained that they should be shaped to the likeness of his Son, that he might be the eldest among a large family of brothers (Romans 8,29).

children of His Father because we are united so intimately and vitally to God's only begotten Son. We become children of God only when united to Christ, for then God looks at us and sees His Son. Apart from union with Christ we could not say, in the fullest meaning of the term, "Our Father."

He destined us—such was his will and pleasure—to be accepted as his sons through Jesus Christ, that the glory of his gracious gift, so graciously bestowed on us in his Beloved, might redound to his praise (Ephesians 1,5–6).

children of His mother, too, for He has given her to be the spiritual mother of all who become His beloved disciples through love.

Jesus saw his mother, with the disciple whom he loved standing beside her. He said to his mother, 'Woman, behold your son.' Then he said to the disciple, 'Behold your mother.' (John 19, 26–27).

co-victors over Satan because we share in the victory which Christ has already won. The prediction in Genesis 3,15 was that the woman's seed would wound Satan in the head. This triumph over Satan was effected through Christ's death and resurrection. We who are united to Christ die and rise sacramentally in baptism. Christ's victory becomes ours, and we, too, crush Satan beneath our heel.

and the God of peace will soon crush Satan beneath your feet. The grace of our Lord Jesus be with you (Romans 16,20).

spiritual descendents of Abraham, and, as such, the beneficiaries of the promises made to Abraham and his seed. God is always faithful to His promises, so those made to Abraham and his seed must come true. They are fulfilled, says Paul, in Christ, the seed of Abraham, and in all who are joined to Him and thereby become spiritual descendants of the patriarch.

For through faith you are all sons of God in union with Christ Jesus. Baptized into union with him, you have all put on Christ as a garment. There is no such thing as Jew and Greek, slave and freeman, male and female; for you are all one person in Christ Jesus. But if you thus belong to Christ, you are the 'issue' of Abraham, and so heirs by promise (Galatians 3,26–29).

united to each other, for we cannot be united individually to Christ without of necessity coming into close union with one another. The preceding citation from Galatians says that we have become "one person in Christ Jesus." Because of this, all points of distinction, be they of race, or social status, or of sex, become unimportant.

After a consideration of the immense benefits which union with Christ has conferred upon us, we can make our own the phrase sung by the deacon at the Easter Vigil celebrating Christ's victory over Satan. Thinking of the grace and spiritual glory that Christ bestowed upon the world through His victory over sin, the deacon chants with joy: "O happy fault, that occasioned such a magnificent Redeemer!"

THE CHURCH

Our individual union with Christ forms us into a group-unit, an organism, which is given various titles in the New Testament. Those baptized into Christ are called the New Israel, God's People, Christ's Church, His Kingdom, His Body. The last three have become the most popular and most frequently used. Our comprehension of the meaning of the work of salvation for us is increased if we consider the essential characteristics of this Church of Christ which is His Kingdom, His Body. What is it like? How does it act? What powers does it possess? How is it related to Christ?

First and foremost, this group-unit is Christo-centric. Christ is the point of union into Whom all are baptized. The center of this union, consequently, is not a doctrine, not a mode of action, not the inspiring hope of a future life; it is not a devotion, not a sacrifice, not a sacrament. It is a Person: Christ Who died and rose and breathes forth the Holy Spirit. Union with Him is the first characteristic of the Church.

This union is described in many different ways in the New Testament. Various authors, in their attempt to plumb the depths of this infinite truth, have produced different analogies. Christ Himself described it as being similar to the life-giving union which the branches have with the vine. Just as the branches are joined to the vine and draw their life and sustenance from it, so too, the Christian in relation to Christ. The emphasis here is on a union which is vital, organic, intimate, absolutely necessary.

I am the real vine, and my Father is the gardener. Every barren branch of mine he cuts away; and every fruiting branch he cleans, to make it more fruitful still. You have already been cleansed by the word that I spoke to you. Dwell in me, as I in you. No branch can bear fruit by itself, but only if it remains united with the vine; no more can you bear fruit, unless you remain united with me (John 15, 1–4).

Union with Christ is also compared to the union of stones built up into a holy temple. In this analogy two points are underscored. The union is solid, and it is a union aimed at the indwelling of God Himself. The Temple of the Old Testament in which the glory of God dwelled is replaced by the living temple which is Christ and those united to Him. In this living temple God is now to be found.

You are built upon the foundation laid by the apostles and prophets, and Christ Jesus himself is the foundation-stone. In him the whole building is bonded together and grows into a holy temple in the Lord. In him you too are being built with all the rest into a spiritual dwelling for God (Ephesians 2,20–22).

Another comparison used by Paul is that which likens the union of Christ and Christians to the intimate and loving union of man and wife. This is a magnificent, yet daring, comparison. Of all human unions, that between man and wife is the most personal, the most joyful, the most productive of life. Christ and His Church, says Paul, are its model. They form a union which is even more personal, more joyful, more productive of life. No more marvelous commentary on the ideal of the married state can be imagined. Nor could any better human analogy be found to demonstrate the creative love which is the basis for the union between Christ and His Church.

Wives, be subject to your husbands as to the Lord; for the man is head of the woman, just as Christ also is the head of the church. Christ is, indeed, the Saviour of the body; but just as the church is subject to Christ, so must women be to their husbands in everything. Husbands, love your wives, as Christ also loved the church and gave himself up for it, to consecrate it, cleansing it by water and the word, so that he might present the church to himself all glorious, with no stain or wrinkle or anything of the sort, but holy and without blemish. In the same way men also are bound to love their wives as they love their own bodies. In loving his wife a man loves himself. For no one ever hated his own body; on the contrary, he provides and cares for it; and that is how Christ treats the church, because it is his body, of which we are living parts. Thus it is that (in the words of Scripture) 'a man shall leave his father and mother and shall be joined to his wife, and the two shall become a single body'. It is a great truth that is hidden here. I for my part refer it to Christ and to the church, but it applies also individually: each of you must love his wife as his very self; and the woman must see to it that she pays her husband all respect (Ephesians 5,22–33).

Above all, and most strikingly, the union between Christ and Christians is described as body-union with the risen Christ. Paul calls Christians the members of Christ's body, or, simply, Christ's body. What does he mean by this? Basically his idea is that Christians, through union with the risen body of Christ, become members of that body in the sense of being united to it. Consequently, he often speaks of Christ's body when he means both Christ Himself and His Christian members. This is what we now term Christ's Mystical Body. Perhaps the simplest formula to use in understanding this would be something similar to the following: Because we are joined to the glorified risen body of Christ we form His Mystical Body. (The word *body* will hereafter be capitalized when referring to the unity of Christ *and* His human members. It will not be capitalized when referring to Christ's physical body alone.) Christians are Christ's Body, not merely or primarily because they are like a body, but because they are united to a body, the risen body of Christ. A careful study of Paul's description of Christians as the members of Christ or as Christ's Body will show that when Paul speaks in such a manner he always has the thought of the risen body of Christ definitely in mind. Some instances of this are truly striking. The passage we have just seen, Ephesians 5,22–33, is one example. The wife becomes the husband's body by being united physically to that body; the Church becomes Christ's Body by being united spiritually to His risen body through baptism.

Another example is found in the text of 1 Corinthians 6,15–16.

Do you not know that your bodies are limbs and organs of Christ? Shall I then take from Christ his bodily parts and make them over to a harlot? Never! You surely know that anyone who links himself with a harlot becomes physically one with her (for Scripture says, 'The pair shall become one flesh'); but he who links himself with Christ is one with him, spiritually.

Paul's language is startling. He points out that for the Christian there is special malice to the sin of fornication. By such a disordered act, a Christian who is a member of Christ, since he is united to Christ's body, unites himself to the body of a harlot. The language is strong because the facts of the case demand it (Corinth was at that time an infamous center of immorality), but the force of these words underline the realistic fashion in which Paul understood that union with Christ which is the basis of the doctrine of the Mystical Body.

A third example can be found in 1 Corinthians 10,16–17, the

first time Paul explicitly refers to Christians as a Body. The context concerns the Eucharist:

The bread that we break, is it not a sharing of the body of Christ? Because the bread is one, we, though many, become one body, for we all share the one bread.

Paul's thought is this: the bread is the body of Christ. We, though many, become one Body because we partake of the one bread which is one body, Christ's. It is always union with Christ's risen body (even in Eucharistic form) that makes us Christ's Mystical Body.

The whole emphasis of this explanation rests on the truth that the expression "body of Christ" bespeaks in Paul's mind more the meaning of *corporal* than corporate. He never thought of Christ's Mystical Body simply as a corporation, somewhat after the fashion of a religious General Motors or Shell Company. He thought of it with full corporal force as something centered round the glorious and risen body of Christ. The baptismal texts of Paul have the same insistence. For him a man was baptized directly into the corporal Christ, into the Christ Who, having won salvation by His death and resurrection, now pours forth the life-giving Spirit into those united to Him.

Once Paul had established this realistic position it was very natural for him to begin extending this doctrine by a figurative use of it. Being the Body of Christ, Christians could be described in bodylike terms. Certain Christians with authority could be compared to the head, others to the hands, still others to the eyes or the feet. But all of this figurative language was based upon the previous truth of salvation coming through union with Christ's glorified body.

This corporal explanation, we might note, is parallel to the vine-branches analogy found in the Gospel of St. John, chapter

15. In that analogy too, the branches (Christians) are united directly to the vine (Christ), just as for Paul the members (Christians) are united directly to the body (the risen body of Christ). In this intimate union between the risen body of Christ and its members, the Mystical Body, we can say that although the risen body is distinct from the Mystical Body, yet the two are never separate. We Christians are not and cannot be Christ's risen body. Yet so long as we form the Mystical Body, we are never separate from it.

This distinction, but not separation, is underlined by Paul when, in his later epistles (Colossians and Ephesians), he begins to speak of Christ as the Head and of the Church as the Body. The risen body of Christ still forms the center of the unity, but calling Christ the Head makes it clear that no vague pantheism is envisaged. We do not become Christ's risen body: that always remains distinctly Christ's. But we are united to it and by that fact become its members.

This doctrine of the risen Christ and His Mystical Body is related to the other Pauline doctrine of Christ as the New Adam. Our physical descent from the first Adam formed a union with him which brought us death, but our spiritual union with the New Adam has brought us life. In the old Adam humanity fell; united to the New Adam we form a new creation, a resurrected humanity, for the New Adam communicates the life-giving Spirit which makes us His members and brings us to life.

As in Adam all men die, so in Christ all will be brought to life . . . 'The first Adam became an animate being,' whereas the last Adam has become a life-giving Spirit (1 Corinthians 15, 22 and 45).

The second characteristic of Christ's Church-Kingdom-Body is its *Teaching Office*, its continuation of Christ's prophetic ministry as the divine messenger, the living Word of God. It is an office that Christ made firm by promising to send the Holy Spirit as the teacher of truth.

Your Advocate, the Holy Spirit whom the Father will send in my name, will teach you everything, and will call to mind all that I have told you (John 14,26).

The Spirit's "calling to mind" was surely meant to enable the apostles to pass on the instructions and doctrines of Christ to the Christians who would be entrusted to their care. The conclusion to Matthew's Gospel insists on this.

Full authority in heaven and on earth has been committed to me. Go forth therefore and make all nations my disciples; baptize men everywhere in the name of the Father and the Son and the Holy Spirit, and teach them to observe all that I have commanded you. And be assured, I am with you always, to the end of time. (Matthew 28, 18–20).

The apostles exercised this commission and authority from the earliest days of the Church. The first Christian community, that living in Jerusalem after Jesus' ascension, grouped together in an intimate social life in which the apostles' teaching held a central position.

Then those who accepted his word (Peter's on Pentecost) were baptized, and some three thousand were added to their number that day. They met constantly *to hear the apostles teach*, and to share the common life, to break bread, and to pray (Acts 2,41–42).

In carrying out this command to preach what Christ had taught, the infant Church was confident that she possessed, as Christ had promised, the Advocate or the Spirit of Truth, as her divine aid. A sign of such confidence is evident in the decree of

the Council of Jerusalem concerning the Gentile Christians' freedom from the demands of the Mosaic Law. The apostles are
certain that they are enlightened by the Spirit in their teaching.

It is the decision of the Holy Spirit, and our decision, to lay no
further burden upon you beyond these essentials . . . (Acts 15,28).

Paul is certain that as an apostle he too speaks with the power
of Christ and with the help of the Spirit of Truth. In fact, it is
Christ Who speaks in Him.

I am speaking the truth as a Christian, and my own conscience, enlightened by the Holy Spirit, assures me it is no lie . . . (Romans 9,1).

Then you will have the proof you seek of the Christ who speaks
through me, the Christ who, far from being weak with you, makes his
power felt among you (2 Corinthians 13,3).

The Spirit-inspired Church soon formulated this teaching of
Christian truth (Christ's words and deeds, plus the explanation
and application made of them by the apostles, the prophets, and
evangelizers) into the Book of the New Testament. The Spirit-
Living Church produced the book, and the Spirit-Living Church
continues down the centuries to explain the depth of its meaning,
to apply it to the needs and problems of the times, and to
measure her own conduct by it. In all of this, Christ's Church, His
Body, is continuing to exercise the prophetic ministry which was
His. Christ continues to teach in the Church which is His Body,
the extension of the Incarnation in the world.

The third characteristic of the Church is its possession of the
power of Christ. This power was exercised by Christ to overcome Satan and to bring the life of the Spirit into the world.
During His lifetime He began to share it with His apostles. We
have already noted (page 156) that Christ sent the apostles out

to cure sickness and to expel Satan. However, the deepest sharing was made in connection with Christ's death, His resurrection, and His departure from this world. At the Last Supper, in conjunction with the sacrificial changing of the bread and wine into His body and blood, Christ told the apostles to continue this rite and gave them power to do so.

For the tradition which I handed on to you came to me from the Lord himself: that the Lord Jesus, on the night of his arrest, took bread and, after giving thanks to God, broke it and said: 'This is my body, which is for you; do this as a memorial for me.' In the same way, he took the cup after supper, and said: 'This cup is the new covenant sealed by my blood. Whenever you drink it, do this as a memorial of me.' For every time you eat this bread and drink the cup, you proclaim the death of the Lord, until he comes (1 Corinthians 11,23–26).

The power to re-present the unique sacrifice of Christ by which He overcame sin through the supreme practice of love and obedience is thus given to the apostles.

A further sharing in Christ's power is connected with His appearance in the upper room late in the evening of the first Easter Sunday. Glorious in body, communicative of the Spirit, He gives the apostles a participation in the most important of His powers over Satan, that of forgiving sin and of restoring man's vital union with God. Previously the apostles had been able to expel Satan from physical control over a body, and to cure the sickness which sin had brought into the world. Now they are given a power which is truly divine, one most intimately connected with the task of saving man from the kingdom of Satan.

Late that Sunday evening, when the disciples were together behind locked doors, for fear of the Jews, Jesus came and stood among them. 'Peace be with you!' he said, and then showed them his hands and his

side. So when the disciples saw the Lord, they were filled with joy.
Jesus repeated, 'Peace be with you!' and then said, 'As the Father
sent me, so I send you.' He then breathed on them, saying, 'Receive
the Holy Spirit! If you forgive any man's sins, they stand forgiven;
if you pronounce them unforgiven, unforgiven they remain. (John 20,
19–23).

Finally, toward the end of His bodily existence on earth, Christ
gives the apostles that solemn commission whereby His authority
and power become theirs.

Full authority in heaven and on earth has been committed to me.
Go forth therefore and make all nations my disciples; baptize men
everywhere in the name of the Father and the Son and the Holy
Spirit, and teach them to observe all that I have commanded you. And
be assured, I am with you always, to the end of time (Matthew 28,
18–20).

By means of this sharing of His power with chosen intimates,
Christ continues to do now in His Mystical Body what He did
originally in His own physical body. One should receive the
sacraments and meditate upon them with this in mind. The power
of the sacraments is not magical; it is Christ's. Christ shared this
power with men, and it is especially in the sacraments that it is
exercised. Through them Christ continues to forgive sin, to overcome Satan at the heart of his conflict with men and the kingdom
of God. This power to forgive sin is Christ's alone. Chosen men
are used as His instruments to make decisions, to speak the
words of forgiveness and encouragement which Christ did
through His human nature while on earth. But, always, it is Christ
Who acts. When the priest forgives sins, Christ forgives.

Through the sacraments Christ continues to cure the sick. This
is the most obvious purpose of the sacrament of Anointing. It is
a sacrament of healing. For too long this sacrament has been

considered a sacrament of the dying, thus its common name "Extreme Unction." It is much more exact to say that the sacrament of the dying is not properly the Anointing, but Viaticum, the Eucharist given to prepare the dying for their journey into the next world. The direct object of the Anointing is sickness, which it either cures or sanctifies. Nor is it surprising to find that this sacrament of physical healing is also connected in some way to the forgiveness of sins, for both sin and sickness are introduced into the world by Satan. In the sacrament of Anointing, Christ's power flows out through the men who possess it and the kingdom of Satan, of sin and sickness, is again under attack.

Is anyone of you sick? Let him call in the presbyters of the Church. Have them pray over him and anoint him with oil in the Lord's name. And this prayer, rising from faith, will cure the sick person, and the Lord will put him back on his feet. And if he is guilty of sin, he will be forgiven (James 5,14–15).

Through the sacraments Christ continues to send down the Holy Spirit on those whom He has chosen to bear witness to Him. This witnessing to Christ is the special effect of the bestowal of the Spirit, and differentiates it from the other bestowals of which Scripture speaks. We know, for example, that the Holy Spirit is communicated at baptism by the glorified body of the risen Christ to Whom the Christian is united. We also know that the Holy Spirit had been given the apostles before the Feast of Pentecost, since they had received the Spirit to enable them to forgive sins on the night of Easter Sunday. But the bestowal of the Spirit again on Pentecost was meant for a special effect, to make the first disciples ardent and courageous witnesses to Christ, in particular to His resurrection. Christ continues to send the Spirit to make courageous witnesses of the Christians of today through the sacrament of Confirmation.

But you will receive power when the Holy Spirit comes upon you; and you will bear witness for me in Jerusalem, and all over Judaea and Samaria, and away to the ends of the earth (Acts, 1,8).

Peter's sermon on Pentecost speaks clearly of this testifying to Christ.

The Jesus we speak of has been raised by God, as we can all bear witness. Exalted thus with God's right hand, he received the Holy Spirit from the Father, as was promised, and all that you now see and hear flows from him (Acts 2,32–33).

The Pentecostal gift of the Spirit transformed the apostles into witnesses brave enough to lay down their lives for their belief in Christ, the supreme witnessing of martyrdom. The Christian of every age is called to bear similar testimony. From Christ he receives the Holy Spirit in Confirmation to strengthen him for the task.

Through the sacraments Christ continues to offer to the Father the loving and obedient sacrifice of His body and blood. Paul's First Epistle to the Corinthians makes it clear that the Mass was considered a sacrifice from the earliest days of the Church. This Epistle was written about the year 56 A.D., and in its tenth and eleventh chapters Paul speaks of the liturgy of the body and blood of Christ which we call the Mass. In chapter ten, verses 14–21, for example, he calls it vastly superior to the sacrifices of the Gentiles and the Jews. In comparing the Mass to these other sacrifices Paul takes it for granted that it is a sacrifice itself. In the eleventh chapter, verses 23–30, Paul speaks of the liturgical chalice as the new covenant in Christ's blood, He thereby emphasizes with Christ and the early Church that the chalice blood of liturgical worship is covenant blood, sacrificial blood. He also shows his awareness that this blood, renewed by consecration at the express command of Christ, has replaced the animal covenant blood of Moses, becoming the blood of the *new* covenant promised by Jeremia 33,33. The work of salvation is constantly renewed in this sacrament particularly. The sacrifice of Christ is made present again at the very moment that the risen body of Christ appears on the altar. Sacrificial death and glorious resurrection are joined in one. The Christian participates in both of Christ's saving actions by joining himself in sacrifice with Christ and by receiving the body of his risen Lord at the communion table. Joined to his Lord he is joined to his God and to his neighbor. Here is salvation in the concrete. The cause of salvation is re-presented, Christ's sacrificial death and His risen body. Salvation's purpose is realized at the same time, the union of man to man in Christ, and in Christ with God.

Through the sacrament of Holy Orders Christ continues to share His power with the men whom He has chosen to be His living instruments. These are the men to whom Christ has revealed the whole of His truth, the men whom He has personally chosen to bear fruit in His name by harvesting human beings into salvation.

I call you servants no longer; a servant does not know what his master is about. I have called you friends, because I have disclosed to you everything that I heard from my Father. You did not choose me: I chose you. I appointed you to go on and bear fruit, fruit that will last; so that the Father may give you all that you ask in my name (John 15,15–16).

Sharing in Christ's power so intimately sets these men apart from all others. By virtue of Christ's choice they are the men through whom Christ continues to act. They are His human instruments for forgiving sins, for curing sickness, for representing the sacrifice. Through them He continues to overcome Satan and to communicate the life of the Spirit. Because Christ brings people into life, or back to life, through them, they are, in Christ, spiritual fathers.

You may have ten thousand tutors in Christ, but you have only one father. For in Christ Jesus you are my offspring, and mine alone, through the preaching of the Gospel (1 Corinthians 4,15).

Of the men to whom Christ gave His power, one especially was singled out. To this man, Simon Bar-Jona, Christ gave special functions and special responsibilities. Scripture gives us one magnificent description of Simon's elevation to a position of preeminent responsibility and authority. The context is that of Simon's profession of faith in Jesus as the awaited Christ, the promised Messiah. This marked an important step in the process by which the apostles gradually understood who this Jesus of Nazareth was with Whom they had experienced so many amazing things. They had begun to follow Him because of His magnetic personality. They had marvelled at His teaching and at His ability to read human hearts and minds. They had been amazed at His miraculous cures, and dumbfounded at His control of the wild forces of nature, the winds and the storms. They had seen water changed to wine; bread had multiplied in their hands; Lazarus had walked out of his tomb while they watched in terror. When Christ finally asks them what they think of Him, it is Simon who answers in the name of all. They are convinced that He is the Christ whom all Israel has been awaiting. Matthew tells us that Simon's profession merited a mighty response from our Lord. He changes Simon's name to *Rock, Kefa* in the original Aramaic and *Petros* in the Greek translation of it. (So far as we can discover, this term, rock, had never been used as a proper name in either the Aramaic or Greek before Jesus gave it to Simon to symbolize the essential role which would be his in relation to the Church.) *Rock,* he was called, since the Church would be established upon him. At the same time this Rock receives the keys to the Kingdom, the Church. With this, Simon is constituted the foundation of the Church and the living and personal center of its supreme authority. |

When he came to the territory of Caesarea Philippi, Jesus asked his disciples, 'Who do men say that the Son of Man is?' They answered. 'Some say John the Baptist, others Elijah, others Jeremiah, or one of the prophets.' 'And you,' he asked, 'who do you say I am?' Simon Peter answered: 'You are the Messiah, the Son of the Living God.' Then Jesus said: 'Simon son of Jonah, you are favoured indeed! You did not learn that from mortal man; it was revealed to you by my heavenly Father. And I say this to you: You are Peter, the Rock; and on this rock I will build my church, and the forces of death shall never overpower it. I will give you the keys of the kingdom of Heaven; what you forbid on earth shall be forbidden in heaven, and what you allow on earth shall be allowed in heaven' (Matthew 16,13–19).

Nor are these the only responsible roles given to Peter. In the last chapter of John's Gospel still another is indicated. As Christ prepares to leave this world He entrusts Peter with another momentous function, that of being the Good Shepherd in His own place. On this occasion Peter confesses his love for Christ three times, thereby making public confession of his previous triple denial. After every profession of love he is told by Christ to watch over the sheep which the Lord is leaving behind.

After breakfast, Jesus said to Simon Peter, 'Simon son of John, do you love me more than all else?' 'Yes, Lord' he answered, 'you know that I love you.' 'Then feed my lambs,' he said. A second time he asked, 'Simon son of John, do you love me?' 'Yes, Lord, you know I love you.' 'Then tend my sheep.' A third time he said, 'Simon son of John, do you love me?' Peter was hurt that he asked him a third time, 'Do you love me?' 'Lord,' he said, 'you know everything; you know I love you.' Jesus said, 'Feed my sheep' (John 21,15–17).

By Christ's express designation Peter is singled out; he is appointed the Rock, the Keeper of the Keys, the Good Shepherd.

To summarize: the main internal characteristics of Christ's Church are three-fold. By its very nature it is Christo-centric. This is stressed when we speak of it as Christ's Mystical Body, so called because its living members are joined to Christ's glorified body. The Mystical Body is further characterized by its possession of Christ's truth and of His power. Through it Christ continues to teach; through it Christ continues to overcome Satan and to communicate the life of the Spirit. In other words Christ, the center of the Church, His Body, lives on in it in words and deeds. The description of Jesus given us by St. Paul corresponds perfectly with this truth: "He is the *power* of God and the *wisdom* of God" (1 Corinthians 1,24). It is this power and wisdom that the Church, united to Christ through the Spirit, possesses. In the Church one contacts the Savior and experiences salvation, which involves an overcoming of the kingdom of Satan, the negative aspect, and a positive return to the supernatural life, to the original goodness of God which was lost by man's sin. By sin man lost this goodness. Further sin drove him farther and farther from it. With Abraham man started on the way back, and the consummation of this long spiritual journey occurs when Christ has overcome Satan and united men to Himself through the Spirit. At this point, when men united to Christ's risen body form the union of His Mystical Body, man has been restored to the goodness which he had lost.

Christ was innocent of sin, and yet for our sake God made him one with the sinfulness of men, so that in him we might be made one with the goodness of God himself (2 Corinthians 5,21).

8

SALVATION EXTENDED

DURING THE FIRST YEARS after Christ's ascension, the major problem for His followers concerned the nature of the Kingdom of God, the Church. Was it simply a refinement of Judaism, limited to the people of Israel, or was it a new creation inviting into its household all of mankind? This problem was extremely difficult and desperately serious. The story of how it was solved is contained in the Acts of the Apostles, the indispensable source for the history of the primitive Church. Written soon after the facts by Luke who had been involved personally in much of the early missionary work as a close disciple of Paul, it is a book which races enthusiastically through its description of how the Church became extended from Jerusalem to Rome, and how it was led by the Spirit to understand its universal character. It begins with the apostles in Jerusalem hoping for the restoration of the sovereignty of Israel. "Lord, is this the time when you are to establish once again the sovereignty of Israel" (Acts 1,6)? At the conclusion of its story some thirty years later, the Church is firmly established in Rome, heart of the world, and Paul is preaching openly that *"this salvation of God has been sent to the Gentiles: the Gentiles will listen"* (Acts 28,28).

THE CHURCH IN JERUSALEM

The first five chapters of the Acts provide a clear picture of the life of the Church immediately after our Lord's ascension. The followers of Christ formed a closely-knit group headed by the apostles. They led a common life, in which the teaching of the apostles, prayer, and the breaking of bread (the Eucharist) were the main elements. It was a life, too, in which the spirit of brotherly love advanced to the extent that all held their property in common. In this way those who were poor would have their wants taken care of by those who had previously lived in luxury. All of this reminds one of the monastic life which, indeed, is the reproduction down through the centuries of the life led by the first followers of Christ.

They met constantly to hear the apostles teach, and to share the common life, to break bread, and to pray. All those whose faith had drawn them together held everything in common: they would sell their property and possessions and make a general distribution as the need of each required. With one mind they kept up their daily attendance at the temple, and, breaking bread in private houses, shared their meals with unaffected joy, as they praised God and enjoyed the favour of the whole people. And day by day the Lord added to the number those whom he was saving (Acts 2,42–47).

This group, with its common life, had definite leaders, and the Acts speaks clearly of them. There was Peter, the rock of the Church, the other apostles, and the deacons. The whole first half of the Acts is dedicated to a laudatory description of Peter's preeminence. It is he who instigates the election of Matthias to replace Judas. It is he who gives the public sermon on Pentecost; Peter again who heals the cripple and preaches at the Beautiful Gate of the Temple. The two sermons given before the Sanhedrin in chapters four and five are also Peter's, and it is he who is the main figure in the sad incident concerning Ananias and his wife Saphira. Without any doubt, Peter is the leader of the infant Church. The other apostles come next in position of importance. Then come the deacons who are mentioned for the first time in chapter six.

At the same time that the followers of Christ had their own particular community with a unique stamp to it, it is clear that they still participated in the worship and religion of Judaism. We are told of their daily attendance at the Temple in Acts 2,46; of their teaching activity there in 5,42. Their favorite meeting place seems to have been Solomon's Porch just outside the Temple building. And this pinpoints the difficulty. Here was a small group of Jews still connected to Judaism, but at the same time believing that the risen Jesus was indeed the promised Messiah, the Christ. This separated them immediately from their fellow Jews. There they were, one foot inside of orthodox Judaism, the other outside; still practicing Judaism, but certain that it had been fulfilled in Jesus. What was not clear at that moment was whether this perfection of Judaism which Jesus had accomplished was meant to be a simple refinement and elevation of the religion of their fathers, or whether it was a new creation, related to Judaism from which it had sprung, but yet a new covenant, a universal religion. That was the problem. How it was solved is the story which starts with Stephen in chapter six.

STEPHEN AND THE DISPERSAL

Stephen was one of the seven deacons chosen by the apostles to attend to the temporal necessities of the Hellenistic widows. The word *Hellenistic* in this context means those Jews whose background was Grecian. These were people born outside of

Palestine, with Greek as their native tongue, though many of them would have been fluent in Aramaic as well. Stephen, himself, came from such a background. His name is Grecian, and surely his thinking, as manifested in chapter seven, is along very broad lines, not at all what one would expect from a Palestinian Jew, isolated from the influence of international thought. With the appearance of Stephen and his fellow Hellenists, the Church begins to move away from the narrow confines of Judaism and its religious center of Jerusalem. Soon, due directly to Stephen, Hellenistic Jewish Christians would be spreading belief in Jesus outside of Palestine, and to non-Jews. Stephen's importance, consequently, can hardly be exaggerated. His sermon and death constitute a cardinal incident in the Acts.

In the sixth chapter we are told how Stephen's enemies stirred up

false witness who said, 'This man is forever saying things against this holy place and against the law. For we have heard him say that Jesus of Nazareth will destroy this place and alter the customs handed down to us by Moses' (6,13–14).

Indeed, there was some bit of truth to this assertion, though twisted and exaggerated. Stephen certainly believed that both the Temple and the Law were temporary institutions and that their importance had come to an end with the life, death, and resurrection of Christ. He would have stated, also, that Moses, great as he was, must now step aside and give privilege of place to the New Moses, the risen Lord. All of this is seen quite clearly in Stephen's sermon as reported in chapter seven. It is a long one, but it can be reduced to a few fundamental points. By speaking of God's appearance to Abraham in Mesopotamia, Stephen teaches that the activity of God cannot be limited to Palestine of which, Stephen insists, God gave Abraham not a yard. Religion cannot be bound down to one land or one nation. A second point concerns the Temple. It, too, is not necessary. God was well worshipped in the days before the Temple was constructed. And its very construction was the work of Solomon, a man of most doubtful virtue. Finally Stephen points to the sad history of Jewish rejection of the leaders sent her by God. Joseph was ill treated, and so was Moses, and so were the prophets. Not too surprising, then, that Jesus had been betrayed and murdered by the very ones to whom He had been sent. Stephen's point here is not simply that the messengers of God had been persecuted down through history. More important is the truth that God accomplished His plans despite such persecutions, actually by using the persecutions for His own ends. Barely hidden under all this is a subtle reference to Jesus, the last of the prophets to be persecuted, Whose death was simply the prelude to a glorious resurrection.

Stephen's speech is concluded with his description of a heavenly vision. He sees "the Son of Man standing at God's right hand" (Acts 7,56). This declaration of Stephen's faith in the risen Christ seals his fate. He is stoned to death, and those hurling the stones "laid their coats at the feet of a young man named Saul" (7,58).

This is the first instance we have in the history of the early Church of an attempt to detach the religion of Christ from that of Judaism. Not that Stephen scoffed at the latter, he simply pointed out its provisional nature. The time had come, he said, when the value of the Temple and of the Mosaic Law had ceased. In its place had come a religion established by Christ, one which could not be confined to one nation or one country or one sanctuary. His bold speech must have helped his brethren to see a bit more clearly that their new faith was something apart from that into which they had been born.

The death of Stephen had one immediate and far-reaching effect. The wrath of the orthodox Jews was directed fiercely against all such Hellenistic Christians as Stephen. They were driven out of Jerusalem and scattered throughout Judea and Samaria. Some even made their way further north into Phoenicia and Antioch, while others sailed the short distance out to the island of Cyprus. At first these persecuted Christians preached their belief in Jesus to the Jews only, but soon some of them living in Antioch began to preach to the non-Jews as well. And many of these accepted Christ eagerly and sincerely.

This was the beginning of a time of violent persecution for the church in Jerusalem; and all except the Apostles were scattered over the country districts of Judaea and Samaria (8,1).

Meanwhile those who had been scattered after the persecution that arose over Stephen made their way to Phoenicia, Cyprus, and Antioch, bringing the message to Jews only and to no others. But there were some natives of Cyprus and Cyrene among them, and these, when they arrived at Antioch, began to speak to pagans as well, telling them the good news of the Lord Jesus. The power of the Lord was with them, and a great many became believers, and turned to the Lord (11,19–21).

Stephen's intellectual grasp of the new religion was one important item. The practical effect of the persecution which followed his death was still another. The first gave the theology of an independent Christianity. The second spread the Hellenistic Jewish Christians, the more liberal group, far and wide, and it was by this group that the main missionary work was to be done. The Holy Spirit, with Whom Stephen was filled (7,55) was guiding the first Christians with careful hand. The difficult problem concerning the nature of the Church and the position of the non-Jews in it would soon be solved, and each step leading to the solution would be made with the assistance of the Spirit. The first important step was that taken by Stephen.

PETER AND CORNELIUS

The next major step in disclosing the universal character of the Church is described in chapters ten and eleven of Acts. Peter and Cornelius are the principal characters in these chapters. The repeated descriptions of their visions are meant to emphasize the capital importance of the incident, for it was Peter's baptism of the non-Jew Cornelius that created the precedent for the reception of Gentile converts into the Church.

The outline of the account is simple enough. Cornelius, a non-Jew, though interested in Judaism and devoted to the true God, is told in a vision to contact Peter, residing at that time in Joppa. Peter, on his part, receives the famous vision of the sheet lowered down from heaven and containing in it all kinds of creatures, "whatever walks or crawls or flies." When told to kill and eat, he protests that some of the animals there are impure according to the precepts of the Mosaic Law. "It is not for you to call profane what God counts clean," is the divine response. This is, of course, a sign meant to teach Peter that the barrier set up by the Mosaic Law between Jew (the clean) and Gentile (the profane) was abolished.

When the messengers from Cornelius arrive at Peter's dwelling, he is told to accompany them. This advice comes from the Holy Spirit (10,19) Who is directing the whole procedure. Arrived at Caesarea where Cornelius lives, Peter is emboldened by all that has happened to visit Cornelius' non-Jewish household (this, too, was forbidden by Mosaic Law) and, as he preaches Jesus to the people present, the Holy Spirit falls upon the non-Jews. Here was an instance of divine revelation in the concrete. For the

Holy Spirit Himself had entered into non-Jews completely apart from the observance of the Law. Any hesitation that Peter might have had about allowing the Gentiles direct entrance into the Church of Christ vanished. He had them all baptized.

Peter was still speaking when the Holy Spirit came upon all who were listening to the message. The believers who had come with Peter, men of Jewish birth, were astonished that the gift of the Holy Spirit should have been poured out even on Gentiles. For they could hear them speaking in tongues of ecstasy and acclaiming the greatness of God. Then Peter spoke: 'Is anyone prepared to withhold the water for baptism from these persons, who have received the Holy Spirit just as we did ourselves?' Then he ordered them baptized in the name of Jesus Christ (Acts 10,44–48).

This event can well be called the *Pentecost of the Gentiles*. It is interesting to note that Peter presided at both Pentecosts. When he returned to Jerusalem, however, after baptizing Cornelius and his household, he found that a number of the more conservative Jewish Christians were very disturbed by what had happened. These persons would have been willing enough to have the Gentiles accept Christ, but only after they had first become Jewish converts. Peter's description of what had happened silenced such opposition, for the ultimate decision to baptize the Gentiles had been almost forced on him by the Holy Spirit.

'God gave them (the Gentiles of Cornelius' household) no less a gift than he gave us when we put our trust in the Lord Jesus; then how could I possibly stand in God's way?' When they heard this their doubts were silenced. They gave praise to God and said, 'This means that God has granted life-giving repentance to the Gentiles also' (Acts 11,17–18).

This event, directed from beginning to end by the Holy Spirit, was the second act (Stephen's martyrdom was the first) in the unfolding of God's *complete* plan of salvation, one which must include the Gentile as well as the Jew. For the two must be united together in Christ, and in Christ with God. There would still be doubts, hesitation, resistance on the part of those whose Judaism was more vital than their Christianity, but the Holy Spirit was steadily leading the infant Church to an ever deeper and clearer understanding of her catholic self.

PAUL OF TARSUS

Paul, whose Jewish name was Saul, was, like Stephen, a Hellenistic Jew. He was born outside of Palestine in Tarsus, now a part of modern Turkey. He has often been called the midwife of Christianity, the one mainly responsible for cutting the cord binding Christianity to Judaism. This is somewhat of an exaggeration since other men such as Stephen and Peter contributed so much to the constantly clarifying vision of a non-Jewish Christianity. Yet it must be happily admitted that Paul's role in this religious drama was of paramount importance. His conversion to Christ was one of the outstanding occurrences in the religious history of the world. St. Luke considers it so important that he inserts three descriptions of it into his relatively short work. In Luke's eyes, Paul was without doubt the hero of heroes among the first Christians.

The different accounts of Paul's conversion all stress the point that he has been chosen to bring Christ to the Gentile world. Ananias is told that Paul is to be God's chosen instrument to bring the name of Jesus before nations and their kings (Acts 9,15). Paul himself tells us that at the time of his conversion he was called to be a witness to Christ before the world, one sent to open the eyes of the Gentiles, to turn them from darkness to light, from the dominion of Satan to that of God (22,15; 26,17–18). The first years after his sudden and completely unexpected conversion were spent in obscurity. There was the initial three-year period passed in the desert of Arabia and in Damascus. This was followed by a two week stay in Jerusalem. Paul's arrival there was inauspicious. The Christians did not know what to make of him. When last seen some three years before he had been a rabid persecutor of the Faith, and it was hard to believe that such a man could have become a true Christian in the meantime. Only through the intercession of Barnabas, a revered Hellenistic Jewish Christian, was Paul introduced to the apostles. This visit was very short. If the Christians were suspicious of Paul, his former Jewish companions were absolutely irate at what they considered a shameful apostasy. He was forced to leave Jerusalem and Palestine to return to Tarsus.

Paul's positive contribution to Christianity began some years later, four or five perhaps. In the meanwhile, Barnabas had been sent to Antioch to supervise the evangelization going on there, one which included the Gentiles as well as the Jews.

When he arrived and saw the divine grace at work, he rejoiced, and encouraged them all to hold fast to the Lord with resolute hearts; for he was a good man, *full of the Holy Spirit* and of faith (11,23–24).

When Barnabas realized the amount of good that could be done working with both Gentiles and Jews at Antioch he thought of Paul. There was talent, fiery zeal, a brilliant intellect being wasted! So off went Barnabas to Tarsus where he found Paul and brought him back to Antioch.

For a whole year the two of them lived in fellowship with the congregation there, and gave instruction to large numbers. It was in Antioch that the disciples first got the name of Christians (11,26).

Then for a period of some four years, from about 45–49 A.D., Paul and Barnabas were out on the road and on the sea. This was the period of their first missionary journey, one which led from Antioch over to the island of Cyprus, and then north into Asia Minor. Luke insists that this, too, was instigated by the Holy Spirit.

While they were keeping a fast and offering worship to the Lord, the *Holy Spirit* said, 'Set Barnabas and Saul apart for me, to do the work to which I have called them.' Then, after further fasting and prayer, they laid their hands on them and let them go. So these two, sent out on their mission by the *Holy Spirit*, came down to Seleucia, and from there sailed to Cyprus (13,2–4).

Luke narrates that Paul, like Stephen and Barnabas, equally catholic-minded pioneers, was "filled with the Holy Spirit" (13,9) during the course of his labor. This first journey resulted in the meaningful experience that the Jews resisted the preaching of the gospel while the Gentiles accepted it sincerely and in large numbers. Everywhere Paul and Barnabas went it was the same story. They would begin by preaching to the Jews for in the plan of salvation the faith was to be offered to them first as the original People of God. When the Jews resisted the offer, the missionaries then turned to the Gentiles where they found a ready and enthusiastic audience. Surely this practical experience convinced Paul that the future of Christianity lay with the Gentiles. Not that he gave up hope for his own people, but he realized that according to the unfathomable mind of God the Gentiles were to enter into the Church before the Jews and, seemingly, in preference to them. All this stands out very clearly in the account of Paul's experience at Pisidian Antioch. The Jews there contradict Paul and Barnabas' preaching and inspire a persecution against them. Thus, the missionaries perforce turn their attention to the

Gentiles. In all this it is *revelation through the Holy Spirit* and the *practical knowledge acquired through bitter experience* that are clarifying the catholic nature of Christ's Church in the minds of those who are preaching the gospel

On the following Sabbath (in Pisidian Antioch) almost the whole city gathered to hear the word of God. When the Jews saw the crowds, they were filled with jealous resentment, and contradicted what Paul and Barnabas said, with violent abuse. But Paul and Barnabas were outspoken in their reply. 'It was necessary,' they said, 'that the word of God should be declared to you first. But since you reject it and thus condemn yourselves as unworthy of eternal life, we now turn to the Gentiles. For these are our instructions from the Lord: 'I have appointed you to be a light for the Gentiles, and a means of salvation to earth's farthest bounds.' When the Gentiles heard this, they were overjoyed and thankfully acclaimed the word of the Lord, and those who were marked out for eternal life became believers. So the word of the Lord spread far and wide through the region. But the Jews stirred up feeling among the women of standing who were worshippers, and among the leading men of the city; a persecution was started against Paul and Barnabas, and they were expelled from the district (13,44–50).

It is interesting to note at this juncture the fact that Paul applies to himself the "light to the Gentiles" vocation predicted in Second Isaia of the Suffering Servant of Yahweh. Paul knows very well that Christ Himself was the Servant Who by His expiatory death satisfied for the sins of men. But he also knows that Christ lives in him, using him as a personal instrument for spreading the light of Christianity into the darkness of the Gentile world.

By the time this first journey had come to an end, the issue of the universal nature of Christianity was perfectly clear in the mind of Paul. Christ's Church was catholic. All were invited into it, Jew and non-Jew alike. And, strange and paradoxical as it certainly seemed, it was the non-Jewish world which was flocking in. This had an important side effect upon Paul's thinking, too. The second coming of Christ (the *parousia*) was to follow the entrance of the Jews into the Church. Paul now realized that the Gentiles were called to enter before the Jews. This fact pushed the *parousia* far off into the future. As a result, Paul and the other Christians were encouraged to concentrate more upon the important sources of supernatural life in the Church which would be their support during the long wait for the final coming of Christ.

Upon their return to Antioch, Paul and Barnabas related their experiences to their fellow Christians. Happily they reported that the success which the Church at Antioch had enjoyed in preaching to the Gentiles had been duplicated during their own voyage. The conclusion of all was that the gates of faith, according to the designs of God revealed through the Holy Spirit, opened wide to the Gentiles.

When they arrived (back in Antioch) and had called the congregation together, they reported all that God had helped them to do, and how he had thrown open the gates of faith to the Gentiles (14,27).

The picture was clearing. *The* problem of the early Church was almost solved.

THE COUNCIL OF JERUSALEM

The various steps by which Stephen, Peter, Paul and Barnabas, all aided by the Holy Spirit, cast light on the catholicity of the Church reached their proper goal in the Council of Jerusalem in the year 50 A.D. The Council was provoked by the intransigent attitude of Jewish Christians of pharisaic, ultra-orthodox Judaic background. These insisted that the Gentile converts "must be circumcised and told to keep the Law of Moses" (15,5). The theology of Stephen, the baptism of Cornelius by Peter, the experiences of Paul and Barnabas were all opposed to such a myopic interpretation of Christianity, but, in fairness, it is not too difficult to see why this Jewish attitude toward the necessity of the Mosaic Law took a long time to die. The long tradition of over 1200 years extending back to the time of Moses had established customs and prejudices that could not be extinguished in a few months or a few years.

The Christians of Antioch were especially disturbed by the vigor with which the Jewish Christians, favoring the necessity of the Mosaic Law, pushed their claims. Antioch sent a delegation headed by Paul and Barnabas to Jerusalem to seek an official apostolic ruling on this supremely critical matter. During the meeting there, commonly called the Council of Jerusalem, the experiences of Peter, Paul, and Barnabas were the deciding factors. Peter recalled how the Holy Spirit had been given to Cornelius and his household, the Spirit making no distinction between Jews and non-Jews in the bestowal of His gifts. Barnabas and Paul followed with a description of the miracles that God had worked for the Gentiles during their travels. A final summation and conclusion was given by James, Bishop of Jerusalem and a relative of our Lord. Tradition speaks of this man as a conscientious observer of the Law, one to whom even the pharisaic fringe would listen. His conclusion insofar as the Gentiles were concerned, was the same as that of the first three speakers. The Gentiles turning to the Lord do not fall under the restrictions of the Mosaic Law. In the interest of peace and unity, however, he recommends that they obey at least those prescripts which the book of Leviticus (chapters 17–18) had already established for Gentiles living in Palestine, namely, that they avoid food offered to idols, meat from which the blood had not been

properly drained, and marriage within the degrees forbidden by
Jewish Law. These prescripts listed by James should be regarded
as a practical compromise on non-essentials. That concerning the
blood, for example, made social contact between Jewish and
Gentile Christians a simpler affair to manage. Jewish Christians
could thereby share the table with Gentiles without being of-
fended or nauseated by the presence of foods against which they
were mentally and physically prejudiced. The concluding decree
of the Council is striking because of its manifest belief in the
abiding assistance of the Holy Spirit during its deliberations.

We, the apostles and elders, send greetings as brothers to our
brothers of gentile origin in Antioch, Syria, and Cilicia. Forasmuch as
we have heard that some of our number, without any instructions
from us, have disturbed you with their talk and unsettled your minds,
we have resolved unanimously to send to you our chosen representa-
tives with our well-beloved Barnabas and Paul who have devoted
themselves to the cause of our Lord Jesus Christ . . . *It is the decision
of the Holy Spirit, and our decision to lay no further burden upon
you beyond these essentials* . . . (Acts 15, 23–28).

And then follow the three recommendations made by James and
the others.

With this teaching of the Council of Jerusalem, the Holy Spirit
has, over the short period of twenty years, given the solution to
the Gentile problem. Stephen had contributed his share to the
solution, so had Peter and Paul and Barnabas. But throughout the
whole process it was the Spirit Who inspired the various characters in the roles they had to play. With the doors of the Church
now opened wide to the Gentiles, Paul and the other missionaries
hurried off by highway and sea to spread the gospel of Christ.
The salvation accomplished by Christ, to be shared in through
union with Him, was now extended on terms of equality to both

Jew and Gentile. All was in readiness for the centuries-long task and vocation of making the world one in Christ and, in Christ, one with God. All men were being invited back to the original goodness of God which man possessed before the sin of the First Parents.

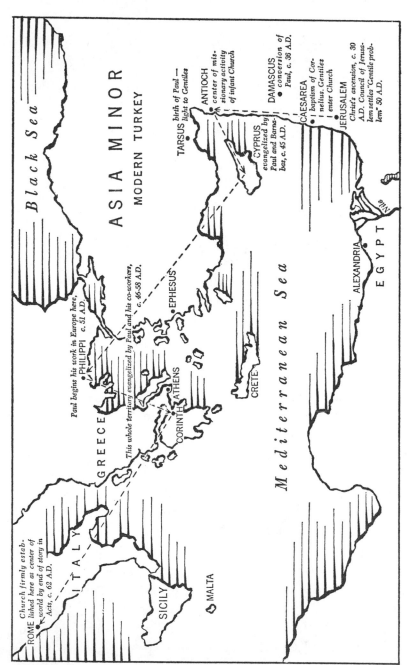

Black Sea

ASIA MINOR

MODERN TURKEY

TARSUS *birth of Paul — light to Gentiles*

ANTIOCH *center of missionary activity of infant Church*

DAMASCUS • *conversion of Paul, c. 36 A.D.*

CAESAREA I *baptism of Cornelius. Gentiles enter Church*

JERUSALEM *Christ's ascension, c. 30 A.D. Council of Jerusalem settles "Gentile problem" 50 A.D.*

CYPRUS *evangelized by Paul and Barnabas, c. 45 A.D.*

This whole territory evangelized by Paul and his co-workers, c. 46-58 A.D.

EPHESUS

Paul begins his work in Europe here, c. 51 A.D. • PHILIPPI

GREECE

CORINTH • ATHENS

CRETE

Mediterranean Sea

ALEXANDRIA

E G Y P T

ITALY

Church firmly established here as center of world by end of story in Acts, c. 62 A.D. ROME •

SICILY

MALTA

Nile

SPREAD OF THE CHURCH: HER CATHOLIC CHARACTER

9

CHRISTIANITY AND JUDAISM

RELATIONSHIP BETWEEN THE TWO

WE HAVE SEEN that God established two formal covenants, two formal religions in the world. The first was that given by Moses, the Old Covenant which came into existence on Mount Sinai. The second was inaugurated by Christ, the New Moses, on the Mount of Beatitudes and ratified by the blood of Calvary. As the end of this treatment of salvation nears, it seems necessary to say something about the relationship between the two. For there *is* a relationship, a very definite one. Christ, though born of a virgin, thus indicating a break between New and Old, was still born a descendant of both Abraham and David. This relates the two religions, and so they were meant to be in the plan of God. But precisely what is the relationship?

Here, again, we must turn to *the* theologian of the New Testament writings, St. Paul. For him, as a former pharisee trained for long years to know and love the Mosaic Law, this question was of deep interest. He explains the connection between Judaism and Christianity in a number of different ways, all of which taken together give the whole picture.

First of all, Judaism performed the office of a tutor to Christianity. The word *tutor* in this context is, perhaps, misleading. It translates the Greek word which has been taken over into English as pedagogue. To avoid confusion, it must be kept in mind that for the Greeks the pedagogue was the slave who led the child to school. Once he had accompanied the child to the door, his work was done. It is in this sense that Paul terms Judaism the pedagogue or tutor. Its function was to lead the world to the door which is Christ. Once it had served this purpose its work was done, which, of course, is not to disparage the importance of the work it had performed. But, and upon this Paul insists, its work is now ended. The world has been led to Christ: Judaism's day is over.

Thus the law was a kind of tutor in charge of us until Christ should come, when we should be justified through faith; and now that faith has come, the tutor's charge is at an end (Galatians 3, 24–25).

A second explanation compares Judaism to a young c' 'ld' a minor, while Christianity is the son come to age, the adult. During the time that the child is a minor he is treated almost as a slave, guarded and supervised as he is by trustees. The inheritance is promised to him, but he does not possess it and cannot use it. Once he comes of age, however, the situation changes. He is an adult, the matured son, and the heir with power over his inheritance. This is somewhat similar, observes Paul, to Judaism as compared to Christianity. Judaism was always immature, somewhat of a slave since it was encumbered with laws for all situations. Christianity is the adult, free with the freedom of the Spirit, and already in possession of the inheritance, the Spirit given by the risen Lord. Paul, again, does not mean to debase Judaism. After all, the adult is the man that he is because of what he was as a child. In this sense, the "child is father of the man." There is not, and never can be, a complete cleavage between these two periods of human life. The second builds on the first, depends on it, is different from it but essentially related to it.

This is what I mean: so long as the heir is a minor, he is no better off than a slave, even though the whole estate is his; he is under guardians and trustees until the date fixed by his father. And so it was with us. During our minority we were slaves to the elemental spirits of the universe, but when the term was completed, God sent his own Son, born of a woman, born under the law to purchase freedom for the subjects of the law, in order that we might attain the status of sons.

To prove that you are sons, God has sent into our hearts the Spirit of his Son, crying 'Abba! Father!' You are therefore no longer a slave but a son, and if a son, then also by God's own act an heir (Galatians 4,1–7).

It might be of some help at this point to descend to particulars in this attempt to relate these two God-given religions. A partial listing of the related individual elements of each follows:

Old Covenant: the Child

1. Monotheism—the supreme doctrine of Judaism was the existence of one and only one God. This was its unique possession, one of which the surrounding nations had not an inkling.

New Covenant: the Adult

1. The Trinity—this is the supreme truth of Christianity. It does not deny, of course, that there is one God, but adds to that fundamental truth a much deeper knowledge of the divine nature, for it is possessed wholly and equally by three Persons, the Father, Son, and Spirit.

2. The law of the Jews was basically the law of the Ten Commandments. All of these were founded on the virtue of *justice*, the virtue of "mine and thine." Man must give to God what belongs to Him, and not misuse what is His; man must give to his

2. The law of Christ is much more elevated, simpler in a sense, and surely much more difficult. It can be expressed in one word—*love*. This means love of God above all things with all one's being, and love of one's neighbor as himself. The man who loves his neighbor

fellowman what belongs to him, and not steal it, destroy it, or desire it. (Love was also an Old Testament precept, but it was a command severely limited both in theory and practice. It was rarely understood to include non-Jews, much less one's active enemies.)

(and, for the Christian everyone is his neighbor) need not be told that he must not kill him, or steal from him, or run away with his wife. In this sense the law of love renders the Ten Commandments unnecessary.

3. The Jewish sacrifices were concerned with animals and produce. They were holocausts, communion sacrifices, expiations, offerings of incense, bread, or the produce of the fields.

3. The Christian sacrifice is vastly superior to that of the Jews, and, at the same time, includes all the facets of Old Testament sacrifice. Christ's body and blood, the offerings of love and obedience, are the sacrifice of Calvary and that of its re-presentation in the Mass. They are as superior to the Mosaic offerings as the God-Man is superior to brute animals. At the same time, Christ's death was like a holocaust and a sprinkling of blood for expiation. The re-presentation of that sacrifice in the Mass is a communion-sacrifice which employs bread, wine as the produce of the fields, and incense.

4. The proudest boast of the Jews was that they were the sons of God, which they undoubtedly were. This meant that God treated them in fatherly fashion; He acted like a father toward them and they were to obey Him as sons.

4. The Christian's divine sonship is of a higher order. He is son of God in the sense that he is intimately and spiritually united to Christ Who is the natural Son of God. In Christ, *the* Son of God, does he become God's son. God looks at him and sees Christ with Whom he is united.

Old Covenant: the Child
(cont.)

5. The Exodus was God's saving work in the Old Religion. What it effected was salvation from physical captivity in Egypt. Its main elements were the passover blood sprinkled on the doors, and the crossing of the sea.

6. The Exodus food was the manna, the physical bread provided by God during the years in the desert. It conserved man's natural life.

7. The Temple of the Old Law was a building of stones and wood in which God, by His own desire, dwelt during the years that the Ark was enclosed within it. It was also the center of Jewish public worship.

8. The prophet Osee depicted Israel as the bride of Yahweh, a

New Covenant: the Adult
(cont.)

5. Christians, too, had and have an Exodus, a release from captivity, this time from that of sin. It is Christ, the New Moses, Who effects it by the sprinkling of His own blood. We share in this saving work by passing through the waters of Baptism.

6. The Exodus food of Christianity is the bread given by Christ, His own body and blood in Eucharistic form. This conserves and strengthens man's spiritual life during the desert years leading man into the promised land of heaven.

7. Christ Himself has become our temple. He revealed this truth by saying that in three days He could rebuild the temple, speaking of His own body (John 2,21). He is a Temple in the sense that God does and must dwell in Him since He is God. In Him, we become the temple of God. At the same time, it is the Body of Christ in the Eucharist which has become the center of Christian worship. All our liturgy centers around the Mass and the Eucharist.

8. St. Paul also speaks of the Church of Christ as His bride. In

faithless bride, unfortunately, but one with whom God was in love with an inexplicable divine love, one whom God treated as bride. so doing, he adds a new depth of spiritual reality to the concept. Not only does Christ love and treat the Church as a bride, but He unites her to His own risen body through faith, the sacraments, and charity.

The parallel between the child and the adult, as well as the superiority of the latter, comes through clearly in these comparisons. Christianity is everything that Judaism was, but is vastly more than Judaism. The young child has grown into the mature man, possessor of the inheritance.

Paul furnishes a third and final description of the relation of the two religions in terms of the contrast between *promise and fulfillment*. From beginning to end, Judaism was a religion of promise. It always looked to the future, to the days to come when the promises to Abraham, to Moses, to David, and to the prophets would be fulfilled. All of the promises were finally fulfilled in Christ, and they resulted in a new covenant, a new religion. The fact that Christ was the fulfillment of all the promises is stated very vividly and succinctly by Paul.

He is the Yes pronounced upon God's promises, every one of them (2 Corinthians 1,20).

Specifically, how were the promises fulfilled in Jesus?

1. The promise in Genesis 3,15 of the fatal wounding of Satan's head in a conflict in which the woman's seed would be bruised was fulfilled by Christ's death and resurrection. The woman's seed was, indeed, wounded, wounded unto death, but this was Christ's victory over sin to be followed by His resurrection-victory

over the power of death itself. At the very moment when Christ
seemed to be overcome by Satan, just the opposite was true. This
is the divine irony of Christ's death. By taking Christ's life the
kingdom of Satan lost the war. Paul has noted this for us.

I speak God's hidden wisdom, his secret purpose framed from the
very beginning to bring us to our full glory. The powers that rule
the world have never known it; if they had, they would not have
crucified the Lord of glory (1 Corinthians 2,7–8).

2. The promise to Abraham that the nations would be blessed
because of his family was also fulfilled in Christ. Son of Abraham, He has given this blessing to the nations, the non-Jews, who
have been united to Him. These have become, in Him, the spiritual descendants of father Abraham. Paul comments on this
frequently in his Epistles to the Romans and Galatians. His
simplest expression of this truth is given us in one packed verse.

And the purpose of it all (Christ's crucifixion) was that the blessing
of Abraham should in Jesus Christ be extended to the Gentiles, so that
we might receive the promised Spirit through faith (Galatians 3,14).

3. Nathan's promise to David's descendants concerned a kingdom which would be both eternal and universal. The whole of
the Gospel of St. Matthew speaks of this kingdom. The kingdom
is the Church, the Mystical Body of Christ. It is because Christ
did bring this promised kingdom into existence that Matthew insists so often during the first two chapters of his Gospel that Christ
was the son of David. It should be remembered also that Luke's
story of the annunciation refers directly to Mary's Son as the
kingly descendant of David, the one who would possess the
eternal kingdom.

the Lord God will give him the throne of his ancestor David, and he will be king over Israel forever; his reign shall never end (Luke 1,32–33).

This promise concerning the descendant of David, and the preceding one regarding the blessing to the Gentiles were combined in one is Isaia 11,10. Paul quotes Isaia, while noting that Christ is the fulfillment.

Christ became a servant of the Jewish people to maintain the truth of God by making good his promises to the patriarchs, and at the same time to give the Gentiles cause to glorify God for his mercy. As Scripture says . . . 'There shall be the *Root of Jesse*, the one raised up to govern the Gentiles; *on him the Gentiles shall set their hope*' (Romans 15,8–12).

4. Jeremia, too, had made a solemn promise.

The days are coming, says the Lord, when I will make a *new covenant* with the house of Israel and the house of Juda (Jeremia 31,31).

Christ *did* make a new covenant, a new religion. It was sealed like the old covenant had been sealed by Moses. On Mount Sinai Moses had splashed blood on the altar representing God and then upon the people. This was the symbol, the outward sign that God and His people were now of the same family, of the same blood. Christ sealed the new religion with His own blood. When Paul speaks of the tradition concerning the Last Supper which had been handed on to him, he gives us a wording about the wine changed to blood which is almost the same as that used by Moses ("This is the blood of the covenant" Exodus 24,8), but with the addition of the word "new" which refers to Jeremia's prophecy.

In the same way, he took the cup after supper, and said: 'This cup is the *new covenant* sealed by my *blood*' (1 Corinthians 11,25. Hebrews 6,6–13 stresses the same point.)

At the same time that the Eucharistic sacrifice is the sacrifice of Jeremia's promised new covenant, it is also the universal sacrifice promised by Malachia. "From the rising of the sun," that prophet had said, "even to its setting" God's name would be great among the nations. Everywhere they would bring sacrifice and a pure offering to His name. And, in fact, it is the Gentiles who have entered into the religion of Christ and have accepted His sacrifice as their own. Christ commanded at the Last Supper that the memorial of this sacrifice, its re-presentation under the appearances of bread and wine which are in reality His body and blood, be constantly repeated to proclaim His death until the day of His final coming.

This cup is the new covenant sealed by my blood. Whenever you drink it, do this as a memorial of me. For everytime you eat this bread and drink the cup, you proclaim the death of the Lord, until he comes (1 Corinthians 11,25–26).

5. Moses, too, had made a promise concerning a great prophet who was to come. The long line of prophets who followed him were partial fulfillments of this promise, each one being a messenger of God as Moses was. Yet the Jews confidently expected a supreme prophet, one of the stature of Moses himself. When John the Baptist began to preach beyond the Jordan, it was thought that perhaps he was this awaited prophet.

This is the testimony which John gave when the Jews of Jerusalem sent a deputation of priests and Levites to ask him who he was. He confessed without reserve and avowed, 'I am not the Messiah.' 'What then? Are you Elijah?' 'No,' he replied. 'Are you *the prophet we await?*' He answered 'No' (John 1,19–21).

John was not that prophet, but Jesus was. The sermon of Peter on the occasion of the cure of the cripple at the Beautiful Gate of the Temple refers to this fulfillment explicitly.

He (Jesus) must be received into heaven until the time of universal restoration comes, of which God spoke by his holy prophets. Moses said, 'The Lord God will raise up a prophet for you from among yourselves as he raised me; you shall listen to everything he says to you, and anyone who refused to listen to that prophet must be extirpated from Israel' (Acts 3,21–23).

6. Lastly, the prophets had spoken often about a chosen remnant, a small group of faithful Jews, who would survive every catastrophe, every destruction, to carry on the destiny of God's people and to receive the promises made to it. This remnant, too, can be found in Christ, specifically in the small group of Jews who accepted Jesus as Christ and were united to Him. A number of Israelites rejected Jesus to their own loss. But the chosen few, the remnant, received Him as Messiah and Lord. In them are the promises made to Israel accomplished.

In just the same way at the present time a '*remnant*' has come into being, selected by the grace of God . . . What Israel sought, Israel has not achieved, but the *selected few* have achieved it (Romans 11, 5–7).

The two religions are, then, like the young child in comparison to the mature son and heir, like the promise in relation to its fulfillment. Judaism served the important purpose of leading the spiritual destinies of the world to the door which is Christ. The basic difference between the two can be expressed in one word,

Christ. He is what the Old Israel hoped for and desperately needed; He is what the New Israel possesses as its Savior and source of life. How great is the distance between the two religions? As great as Christ Himself! He is the distance! Not that Christians can boast of this as though it were the result of each one's personal worth or merit! Not at all. Christ was a *gift* to the world which did not deserve Him; He is a gift to each individual soul, the supreme gesture of God's love and mercy. Finally, one last observation: Christianity is what Judaism was meant to become. And for this reason, if for no other, Christianity's hand of friendship must always be extended to the Jewish people.

THE MYSTERY OF JUDAISM

There are really two great mysteries regarding Judaism. One is the sad fact that after centuries of waiting for her savior and king, she failed to recognize Him at His coming. That was the major scandal for the first Jewish Christians. How could it be that their Jewish brethren refused to believe in Jesus? Paul undertook to answer this question in chapters nine to eleven of his Epistle to the Romans. The second mystery is more modern. How is it that the Jewish people have managed to continue in group existence over a span of what is now approaching 1900 years without Temple, altar, and sacrifice? This enigma, of course, never presented itself to Paul, and yet with his rare genius he has left us the principle upon which the solution must be based.

Failure to Accept Jesus. First of all, the Jewish failure to accept Jesus as savior, as the awaited Davidic king, must be considered. Paul's grief over this fact is deep, so sincere that it can be felt keenly and vividly in the verses that bare his love for his own people. He is sympathetic to their tragedy to the point of almost willing to be separated from Christ that they might be united to Him. His paramount hope and desire is for their salvation.

I am speaking the truth as a Christian, and my own conscience, enlightened by the Holy Spirit, assures me it is no lie: in my heart there is great grief and unceasing sorrow. For I could even pray to be outcast from Christ myself for the sake of my brothers, my natural kinsfolk. They are Israelites: they were made God's sons; theirs is the splendour of the divine presence, theirs the covenants, the law, the temple worship, and the promises. Theirs are the patriarchs, and from them, in natural descent, sprang the Messiah (Romans 9, 1–5).

Brothers, my deepest desire and my prayer to God is for their salvation (Romans 10,1).

Indeed, the fact that the main body of Judaism was not transformed into Christianity was frightfully difficult to explain. God had made His promises to Abraham, to Moses, to David, to the prophets; promises of a countless progeny, of an eternal and universal kingdom. Was it possible that God was proving unfaithful to these promises? The thought was out of the question.

It is impossible that the word of God should have proved false (Romans 9,6).

God's promises to the descendants of Abraham must be fulfilled. But, Paul would ask, who are the descendants of Abraham for whom the promises have been fulfilled? Are they simply those related to Abraham by natural generation, or are they what we might call Abraham's spiritual children those related to Abraham by their spiritual union with Christ, son of Abraham? Paul's answer is given in Romans 9,8, and it is even more apparent in a parallel passage in his letter to the Galatians.

That is to say, it is not those born in the course of nature who are children of God; it is the children born through God's promise who are reckoned as Abraham's descendants (Romans 9,8).

For through faith you are all sons of God in union with Christ Jesus. Baptized into union with him, you have all put on Christ as a garment. There is no such thing as Jew and Greek, slave and freeman, male and female; for you are all one person in Christ Jesus. But if you thus belong to Christ, you are the 'issue' of Abraham, and so heirs by promise (Galatians 3,26—29).

It is to the Christians, Jew and Gentile both, the *spiritual* descendants of father Abraham, that God has shown His loving mercy. In the plan of salvation they have replaced the Old Israel and assumed her prerogatives. They have become God's sons and His beloved people.

Such vessels are we, whom he has called from among Gentiles as well as Jews, as it says in the Book of Hosea (Osee): 'Those who were not my people I will call My People, and the unloved nation I will call My Beloved. For in the very place where they were told 'you are no people of mine,' they shall be called Sons of the living God' (Romans 9,24–26).

The fact that it is the spiritual children of Abraham, not his physical descendants, that have been chosen fits perfectly into the divine pattern of *election* evident throughout the history of Israel. God continually chose one person in preference to another. He chose Sara's son Isaac, not Agar's child Ismael, though Abraham was father of both children. Of the twins Esau and Jacob, God chose Jacob even though he was the younger. And now, Paul's conclusion would be that He has again made His choice: the spiritual descendants of Abraham in preference to the Jewish people who constitute Abraham's natural progeny. God's reasons for acting in such a way must remain unquestioned. God is God, which means that essentially He remains a mystery to man who cannot understand all that God does, or why He does it. Above all he cannot dare to question God as though the infinite Lord had to reveal to man, His creature, the why and wherefore of His divine deeds. Paul says:

Who are you sir, to answer God back? Can the pot speak to the potter and say 'Why did you make me like this?' Surely the potter can do what he likes with the clay. Is he not free to make out of the same lump two vessels, one to be treasured, the other for common use (Romans 9,20–21)?

But how can it be, the argument runs, that Jesus has not been accepted? Humanly speaking, how can one account for such a strange twist in the destiny of a people? How is it that many Jews failed to accept the message preached to them by the first Christian missionaries, the message of the good news that Jesus was the Christ? Difficult questions, surely, but Paul does his best with them. He, a former pharisee, knows well that the Jews have been zealous, but their zeal has been misdirected and ill-informed. They have placed their hope for salvation in the works of the Law, in their own power to observe the prescripts. This was the basic mistake, for only in Christ can salvation be found. The fundamental union with Christ, the union which alone brings salvation, comes through belief in Jesus, in a firm and witnessed faith in Jesus as risen Lord. Here is the precise point around which the tragedy of the Jews centers. Their human works cannot save them, yet they are zealous for them. Faith in Jesus as risen Lord can save them, yet this they lack.

To their zeal for God I can testify; but it is an ill-informed zeal. For they ignore God's way of righteousness, and try to set up their own, and therefore they have not submitted themselves to God's righteousness. For Christ ends the law and brings righteousness for everyone who has faith . . . If on your lips is the confession, 'Jesus is Lord,' and in your heart the faith that God raised him from the dead, then you will find salvation. For the faith that leads to righteousness is in the heart, and the confession that leads to salvation is upon the lips (Romans 10,2–4. 9–10).

Does this mean that God has rejected Israel, that the Jews no longer have a particular relation to Him? Paul, Jew that he is and ardent lover of his own people, cannot answer this in the affirmative. For one thing, not all Jews have rejected Jesus. The first Christians were all Jews, and in them Paul sees the chosen "remnant" of which the prophets repeatedly spoke. The prophetic idea was that there would never be a tragedy so immense as to eliminate the Jews completely from God's loving protection. This has been verified, notes Paul, even in this fulfillment of Judaism accomplished by Christ. In this instance, too, a faithful remnant of Jews has survived and taken a chosen and unique position in the Christian fulfillment of salvation. Surely in this sense God has not rejected His people.

I ask then, has God rejected his people? I cannot believe it! I am an Israelite myself, of the stock of Abraham, of the tribe of Benjamin. No! God has not rejected the people which he acknowledged of old as his own. You know (do you not?) what Scripture says in the story of Elijah—how Elijah pleads with God against Israel: 'Lord, they have killed thy prophets, they have overthrown thine altars, and I alone am left, and they are seeking my life.' But what does the oracle say to him? 'I have left myself seven thousand men who have not done homage to Baal.' In just the same way at the present time a 'remnant' has come into being, selected by the grace of God. But if it is by grace, then it does not rest on deeds done, or grace would cease to be grace. What follows? What Israel sought, Israel has not achieved, but the selected few have achieved it (Romans 11,1–7).

Paul observes another saving feature in this whole sombre story of the Jewish national tragedy. The one precise point upon which the Jews founder is that which has afforded salvation to the Gentiles, *salvation through faith in Jesus as the risen Lord.* It is as though Jewish blindness has led directly to Gentile light. If every cloud has a silver lining, it is the thought of Gentile salvation through faith in Jesus which constitutes for Paul the consoling aspect of the tragedy now fallen upon the Jewish people. An analogy comes to Paul's mind. The people chosen by God resemble an olive tree. Its original and natural branches were the Jewish people. Now that righteousness comes through faith in Jesus as risen Lord, the natural branches have been lopped off and replaced by others, the Gentiles who have been grafted into the olive tree. The question of faith in Jesus, though it has resulted in the Jews being cut off from the tree, has also effected the grafting in of the Gentiles. This is the bright part of the picture which Paul paints for himself and his readers. But he hastens to warn the Gentiles not to pride themselves over the Jews. The grafting into the olive tree has been a *gift* to the Gentiles, not something that they deserved. Surely their response to this must be one of thanksgiving and one of care lest through faithlessness they, too, be lopped off.

But if some of the branches have been lopped off, and you, a wild olive, have been grafted in among them, and have come to share the same root and sap as the olive, do not make yourself superior to the branches. If you do so, remember that it is not you who sustain the root; the root sustains you. You will say, 'Branches were lopped off so that I might be grafted in.' Very well: they were lopped off for lack of faith, and by faith you hold your place. Put away your pride, and be on your guard; for if God did not spare the native branches, no more will he spare you (Romans 11,17–21).

Jewish Survival. At this point Paul gives himself, his fellow Jewish Christians, and all of us down to the present time, the happy prediction which helps us to solve the other deep mystery concerning Judaism. How, and for what purpose, has it survived down through the centuries? Since the Roman destruction of Jerusalem in the year 70 A.D., the Jews have been without temple, altar, and sacrifice. They were without a country of their own until a few short years ago when Israel was recreated. They have been exiled, driven from land to land, imprisoned in ghettos all over the world, subjected to fierce persecutions, often (may God forgive us) by the very Christians who are their spiritual descendants. And yet they remain. Not even Hitler's satanic persecution could destroy them. In the entire history of the world, no other national group has had such a persistent existence against such immense odds. Jews can make themselves a vital part of any and every nation, yet they still remain a group apart, always conscious of their ancient history, always kept from extinction by the protecting hand of Yahweh. Paul, of course, could not foresee this long history of the Jews which has extended down to our own days. However, he has given us the answer to the mystery. For he confidently expects the day to come when the Jews will accept Jesus as their Christ, as their risen Lord. It is a temporary blindness which covers their eyes, but there is some way in which God's original choice remains firm. When the day comes which God has determined, the original branches will be grafted back into the olive tree. It is a day, surely, to which Paul looks forward in ardent anticipation.

Observe the kindness and severity of God—severity to those who fell away, divine kindness to you, if only you remain within its scope;

otherwise you too will be cut off, whereas they, if they do not continue faithless, will be grafted in; for it is in God's power to graft them in again. For if you were cut from your native wild olive and against all nature grafted into the cultivated olive, how much more readily will they, the natural olive-branches, be grafted into their native stock!

For *there is a deep truth* here, my brothers, of which I want you to take account, so that you may not be complacent about your own discernment: this partial blindness has come upon Israel only until the Gentiles have been admitted in full strength; when that has happened, the whole of Israel will be saved . . . In the spreading of the Gospel they are treated as God's enemies for your sake; but God's choice stands, and they are his friends for the sake of the patriarchs. For the gracious gifts of God and his calling are irrevocable (Romans 11, 22–29).

Only with the conversion of the old Israel to Christ will the work of salvation be fully shared, for only then will there truly be the required union of Jew and Gentile in Christ which is The Mystery spoken of so often by Paul. Until the present day it has been only the remnant of the Jews, the chosen few, who have accepted their divine savior and been united to Him, and in Him to their Gentile brethren. The full effect of Christ's redemptive work, the complete unity which is its purpose, remains unaccomplished till the ancient people of God accept their Messiah. Only then will Paul's grand description of the work of salvation be completely ratified.

Gentiles and Jews, he has made the two one, and in his own body of flesh and blood has broken down the enmity which stood like a dividing wall between them; for he annulled the law with its rules and regulations, so as to create out of the two a single new humanity in himself, thereby making peace. This was his purpose, to reconcile the two in a single body to God through the cross, on which he killed the enmity (Ephesians 2,14–16).

In a singularly true sense will the plan of salvation be accomplished in all of its effects when both the Jews and the Gentiles are finally united, united to each other in Christ, and in Christ united to God and God's goodness. This will bring the circle of the salvation-process to its end where long ago it began, with God and the goodness of God. In the meantime we are all called upon to work with Christ and the Spirit of Christ Who dwell within us to foster in every way possible the progress, spiritual and numerical, of the Kingdom of God on earth, the Church. Only by the spread of the Church which is Christ's Mystical Body will the plan of salvation be brought to completion.

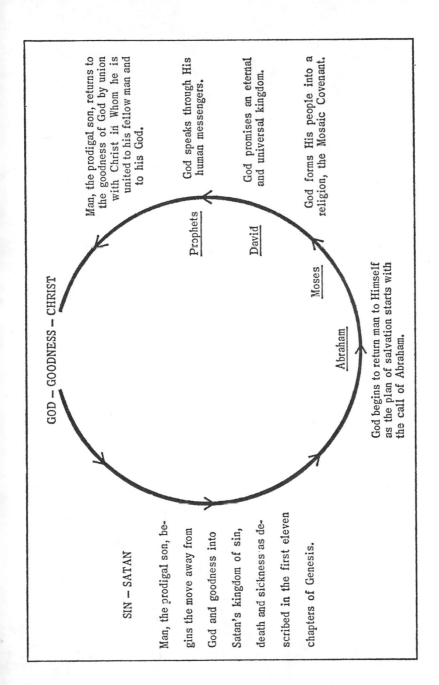

GOD – GOODNESS – CHRIST

Man, the prodigal son, returns to the goodness of God by union with Christ in Whom he is united to his fellow man and to his God.

God speaks through His human messengers.

God promises an eternal and universal kingdom.

God forms His people into a religion, the Mosaic Covenant.

Prophets

David

Moses

Abraham

God begins to return man to Himself as the plan of salvation starts with the call of Abraham.

SIN – SATAN

Man, the prodigal son, begins the move away from God and goodness into Satan's kingdom of sin, death and sickness as described in the first eleven chapters of Genesis.

INDEX